Hampshire

Chris & Jackie Parry

The Horizon Press

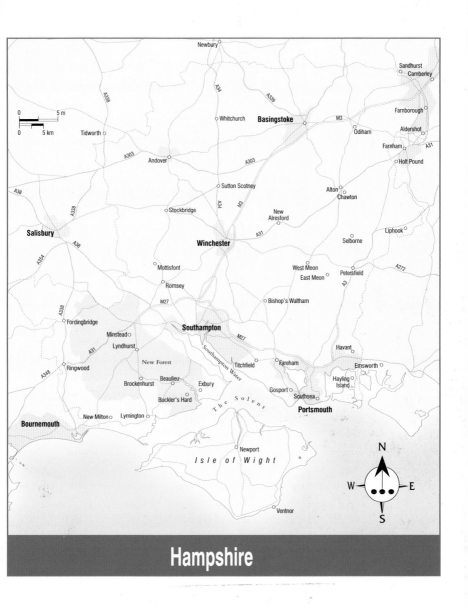

Hampshire

Opposite page: Andover Food Festival

Published by
Horizon Editions Ltd
Trading as The Horizon Press
The Oaks, Moor Farm Road West, Ashbourne, Derbyshire, DE6 1HD
Tel: (01335) 347349 Fax: (01335) 347303
email: books@thehorizonpress.co.uk

Print: Gomer Press Limited. Llandysul, Ceredigion, Wales
Design & Cartography: Michelle Prost

Front Cover: H.M.S. Victory
Back Cover top: Winchester High Street
Back Cover Middle: Fallow Deer
Back Cover Bottom: Wherwell

Picture Credits

Hampshire County Council (www.hants.gov.uk): Back cover top & bottom, 2, 6, 7 mini pic, 7 bottom left, 7 bottom right, 7 top, 10 all, 11 all, 14, 15 all, 18 all, 22 both, 23, 27 all, 30 all, 31 all, 35 mini, 38 bottom left, 38 right, 42, 43, 46, 47, 50, 51 both, 54 top, 55, 63 top, 66 both, 70 both, 71 all, 74 bottom, 75 all, 78, 79 all, 86 all, 87 all, 90, 98 both, 99, 110 both, 115 both, 118, 122, 123 mini pic, 126 both, 127 bottom

Paultons Park (www.paultonspark.co.uk): 7 middle right, 74 top

Breamore House (www.breamorehouse.com): 134

Marwell Wildlife (www.marwell.org.uk): 54 bottom

www.Shutterstock.com (Richard Melichar): 34

Winchester City Council (www.winchester.gov.uk): 34 bottom, 35, 38 top left

Southampton City Council (www.southampton.gov.uk): 58, 62 both, 63 bottom

New Forest Show (www.newforestshow.co.uk): 123 bottom

St Barbe Museum (www.stbarbe-museum.org.uk): 127 middle

New Forest National Park (CMJ Matthews) (www.newforestnpa.gov.uk):
Back cover middle & 127 top

Beaulieu Abbey (www.beaulieu.co.uk): 130

Exbury Gardens (www.exbury.co.uk): 131 top

New Forest Otter, Owl & Wildlife Conservation Park (www.ottersandowls.co.uk): 131 bottom

---

DISCLAIMER
While every care has been taken to ensure that the information in this book is as accurate as possible at the time of publication, the publishers and author accept no responsibility for any loss, injury or inconvenience sustained by anyone using this book.

Contents

Welcome to the
Best of Hampshire **6**
Top Tips 7

1. North Hampshire **14**
Map 15
To the North 23
To the West 26
Places to Visit 32

2. Winchester & the Centre 34
Map 35
Winchester Cathedral 37
Winchester College 40
Wolvesey Castle 40
The Hospital of St Cross 40
Winchester Castle 41
Westgate Museum 43
Military Museums 44
The City Museum 44
High Street 44
Near Winchester 45
To the North 46
To the West 46
To the East 48
To the South-East 53
Places to Visit 55

3. Southampton, Romsey
& the Test Valley **58**
Map 59
Other Highlights 65
St Michael's Church 65
Tudor House Museum 65
Southampton Hall of Aviation 65
Medieval Merchant's House 66
Ocean Village 66
West Quay 66
Civic Centre Art Gallery 66
To the West 66
The Abbey 67

To the East 73
Places to Visit 76

4. Portsmouth & the East **78**
Map 79
Old Portsmouth & the High Street 82
The Historic Dockyard 85
HMS Victory 85
The Royal Naval Museum 88
Southsea 91
Portsmouth City Centre 94
Further Out 95
To the North-West 100
Across The Harbour 100
Gosport Museums 101
To the North-East 107
To the East 111
A Trip down the Meon Valley 114
Places to Visit 119

5. The New Forest **122**
The New Forest Map 123
The Court of Verderers and Traditions
of the New Forest 124
Places to Visit 135

FactFile **137**
Accommodation 137
Cycling 137
Hampshire Farmers Markets 137
Local Producers of Food,
Drinks & Crafts 137
Useful emails 137
Walking 137
North Hampshire 138
Winchester and the Centre 139
Southampton 139
Portsmouth 140
The New Forest 142

Index **143**

Welcome to the
Best of Hampshire

Unless they live in the county, people in Britain always seem to hurry through Hampshire on their way somewhere else: to the Continent, to the Isle of Wight or the West Country. Indeed, Hampshire's main arterial roads, railways and thriving ports encourage people to do so, but those who have the leisure and inclination will be able to discover and enjoy the charms and attractions of a county whose inhabitants are quite content to let others pass them by, if only to keep the well-kept secret to themselves.

Top Tips

1) Highclere Castle

2) Winchester Cathedral

3) Romsey Abbey

4) Longstock Water Gardens

5) Exbury Gardens

6) Paultons Park

7) HMS Victory

8) Portchester Castle

9) View from Portsdown Hill

10) Beaulieu

11) St Mary's Church, Breamore

12) Hurst Castle

1

6

7

5

It is significant that, despite robust opposition by some local families to the policies of Charles I at the time of the Civil War, Hampshire has never been the source for a major rebellion – why would you want to draw attention to all this potential for good living?

Hampshire can also justifiably claim to be the heart of old England. This is emphatically West Saxon country, associated with an unbroken succession of warrior kings whose dynasts grew from petty chieftains in the aftermath of Roman Britain to the great leaders of the re-conquest of the Danelaw in the 10th century. The landscape still retains place-names, churches and features that insistently recall the glory days of Alfred the Great and his successors and the vigorous, now elusive culture of pre-Conquest England. Winchester, the county town, founded by the Romans as Venta Belgarum, was not only the capital of the West Saxon kings, but also, owing to their dominance and that of their Norman successors, the effective capital of England from the 9th to the 12th centuries. With its strategic position on the Channel coast and first-rate communications, as well as the official 'homes' of the Royal Navy and Army at Portsmouth and Aldershot respectively, the county has usually been a front-seat witness to all the major events of the British experience, from the Domesday Book to the modern age. Arthur Mee considered that 'history has made its home in Hampshire'.

The name Hampshire derives from the 'shire of the south-hampton', not to differentiate it from Northamptonshire, but because the town that sprang up and subsequently became Southampton was to the south of the old settlement of Hanton, or Hampton. That is why Hampshire is abbreviated as 'Hants' and not 'Hamps'. The county, the tenth largest in England, is roughly a square with sides of 40 miles (65km) each, not including the Isle of Wight which fits neatly, like a lozenge, into the topography of its coast to the south. This coastline is in fact the county's only natural boundary, for, apart from the minor rivers the Blackwater and the Enborne to the north, the remainder of the shire is defined by the boundaries of the ancient hundreds.

A county of rolling chalk hills, ancient settlements and gentle, well-watered river valleys, Hampshire is famous for its diverse combination of attractive countryside, impressive coastline and picturesque villages. Still managing to preserve a precarious balance between the needs of modern urban development and the sustainability requirements of its farming and rural community, Hampshire has an area of 1,455 square miles (3,769km^2) and, at its widest points, is roughly 55 miles (90km) east–west and 40 miles (65km) north–south. The population of the county is 1.6 million, including the maritime and administratively independent cities of Portsmouth and Southampton. The county contains both the New Forest (a National Park) and a large area of the South Downs, which will shortly become a National Park.

In broad terms, Hampshire is divided into two distinct geological sectors. In the south, the coastal areas of the 'Hampshire Basin', comprising softer clay and gravel, are shielded from the action of the sea by the Isle of Purbeck and the Isle of Wight. These low, flatter landscapes, with their woodland and heath habitats, are typified by the topography of the New Forest, where heath and grassland mixes with coniferous and deciduous trees. As a National Park, the New Forest is protected from excessive use, inappropriate development and agricultural exploitation, while extensive tracts are still open commons grazed by New Forest ponies, cattle and pigs and provide a habitat for wild deer species. Progressive erosion of softer rocks and rising sea levels in the past have formed the estuary of Southampton Water, the large land-locked harbours of Portsmouth and Langstone, together with the Solent separating the mainland from the Isle of Wight.

To the north and at the centre of the county, the underlying rock is predominantly chalk, and high hills slope steeply towards the clay areas to the south. The North and South Downs join together to cut across the north of the county, with some of the chalk hills, such as Beacon Hill, Danebury and White Shoot, rising to almost 1000 feet (300m). Another spine of chalk obtrudes into Hampshire from Sussex just south of Petersfield, passes Butser Hill, the highest point in the South Downs, before separating and heading westwards to Winchester and southwards to the bold ridge of Ports Down, to the north of Portsmouth. Not surprisingly, flint is found in a large number and variety of buildings, both public and private, and the chalk in the soil requires a great deal of moisture. Country lore holds that 'Hampshire ground requires every day of the week a shower of rain,

and on Sunday, twain.'

Even so, Hampshire has a milder climate than the rest of the British Isles, as it is in the far south of the country and enjoys the softening effect of the sea, while being protected from the worst of the south-westerly weather. Temperatures are higher than the UK average at 9.8°C to 12°C (50 to 54°F), with average rainfall at 741–1060 mm (29–42in) per year and higher than average sunshine of over 1,541 hours every year. Hampshire is well stocked with beech and yew trees. Indeed, the yew is known as the 'Hampshire weed' and many will be seen around the county, of which a good many, mostly in churchyards, are over 1,000 years old.

Hampshire's very real and immediate attraction is its variety. The ancient forest and heathland of the New Forest contrast with the remarkable seascapes and tidal inlets of the Solent shore. The chalk downland of the Hampshire highlands is complemented by the South Downs, which in turn are characterised by the wooded slopes and secluded valleys close to the border with Sussex. The whole south coast is dominated by dramatic views of one of the most remarkable, most fortified seaways in the world, a coast that not only contains in Portsmouth Britain's premier naval base, but also in Southampton one of its most famous commercial ports.

The county's distinctive character is, however, defined in the public imagination by its vigorous rivers – the Avon, the Test, the Itchen, the Hamble and the Meon – that weave their way through long-settled, ancient communities, which blend comfortably into the land-

Gilbert White's House

Portsmouth Historic Dockyard

Bucklers Hard

Portchester Castle

Milestones

Manor Farm

Southwick

scape. Over the centuries, Hampshire's way of life, agricultural sustainability and prosperity have depended on these extensive river valleys and the market towns that have thrived in their vicinity. Together with the ports on the coast, they have offered the vital links for

Wellington Country Park

Highclere Castle

commerce and contact with the outside world. In addition, many small ports and inlets along the county's coastline today host a variety of water sports and leisure activities, not least sailing and cruising. However, Hampshire's enduring appeal, as Mary Russell Mitford wrote, 'is not the streams or villages or even the sparkling ocean, but the exquisite arrangement and combination of the whole'.

11

The county is especially famous for its literary connections, most notably Jane Austen at Chawton, Edward Gibbon at Buriton and Gilbert White at Selborne. Portsmouth was home, at one stage or another, to Charles Dickens, George Meredith and Arthur Conan Doyle, while Charles Dibdin, Mary Russell Mitford and Charlotte Yonge were all born in the county. Several notable clerical authors, including Lancelot Andrewes, Charles Kingsley and John Keble also lived in Hampshire and it is likely that Shakespeare kept his head down at Titchfield Abbey after the failure of the Essex rebellion, in which his patron, the Earl of Southampton nearly lost his head.

Hampshire also has more than a passing association with cricket. Hambledon had one of the earliest cricket teams in the country around which much of the modern game was structured and the best bats (endorsed by W.G. Grace) used to be made in Nether Wallop (appropriately!). The author and commentator, John Arlott lived at Alresford for most of his life, with his famous Hampshire burr, reflecting that 'people live there by choice, solely because they like the place'.

For the church enthusiast, Hampshire is – well – pure heaven and almost every town and village has a church of interest or distinction. It has Saxon churches in the Meon Valley that date from the Conversion period of the Dark Ages, a profusion of Norman buildings and later medieval foundations, as well as numerous nationally important churches from more recent times, including the classic Georgian period. Above all, at its heart, in Winchester, it has the longest and, internally, one of the most visually impressive and evocative cathedrals in the country.

Thankfully, amid the pace of modern life, Hampshire manages to hold on to its rural character, even in the vicinity of the great conurbations along the north shore of the Solent and the suburban and light industrial sprawl of the north. Its market towns still retain their distinctive character, while most of its picturesque villages, despite the remorseless advance of barn conversions, intrusive housing development and post office closures, seem able to keep both their distance and community spirit. A recent survey by the magazine Country Life revealed that Hampshire was one of the best counties to live in England and was placed second in a league table after Devon. Each county was assessed on the quality of its health services, green policy, schools, social fabric, heritage, landscape and wildlife, as well as pubs, restaurants, local food and the amount of sunshine hours. More quaintly, it also assessed the number of village greens, the quality of light and peace and quiet, together with the number of residents in Who's Who!

From our point of view both as residents in the county and as people who value the extraordinary inheritance that that has been bequeathed to all of us by previous generations, what follows is the best, in our estimation, that Hampshire has to offer. There is a great deal more to be seen in Hampshire than is indicated, but this guide does not attempt to be a comprehensive gazetteer or to cover the whole county in detail. Our priority has been to highlight the salient features of an attraction and indicate those aspects

Using the guide

For ease of reference, this book has been divided into five geographical sections:

North Hampshire

Winchester and the Centre

Southampton, Romsey and the Test Valley

Portsmouth and the East

The New Forest

These have each been described so that visitors can appreciate either an individual section or select highlights of the five areas as part of a composite tour of the whole county. For each section, ideas for entertainment and excursions have been suggested, together with the top attractions that may be enjoyed there. At the end of the book, readers will find a personal, highly subjective selection of the twelve most representative and must-see attractions and sites in Hampshire; those places that best define the county and its character.

It is perhaps worth saying that Hampshire is unusually well served by its County Council in terms of its tourism, leisure and information services and a great deal of detail is available on the internet about visitor attractions, together with resources to support activities, such as walking, cycling and other outdoor pursuits. The official tourism website www.visit-hampshire.co.uk is a useful resource. It is also worth looking at the country council Hantsweb (www.hants.gov.uk) which is routinely kept up-to-date and is another valuable and accessible way of ensuring that visitors make the best of their opportunities and are able to enjoy to the full what the country has to offer.

which should not be missed. We have given enough historical detail to orientate the visitor, but not too much, we hope, to burden him or her with information that is readily available or discernible on site. Thus, we have not sought to include everything that might be of the slightest interest to the visitor and reader for fear of producing yet another catalogue of 'places to go', but have selected, quite subjectively and in good faith, those sites and experiences that we feel best represent the richness and diversity of this remarkable county. In addition, we are conscious of the wealth of information and access that are available through the Internet and other portable electronic devices. Therefore, we have simply indicated why a particular location or attraction is worth the effort and why it should qualify as something which represents the 'best' of Hampshire. Our hope is that, in using this guide, visitors will be able to explore the county with purpose and pleasure, accumulating their own personal favourites while taking up our suggestions.

1. North Hampshire

The M3 motorway erupts into the north-eastern corner of Hampshire, where the landscape is characterised by the sandy heathland, clay soils and rapidly spreading suburbanisation that is usually associated with the Thames valley. However, it is the east–west A303 that effectively forms the spine across the north of the county, as the motorway veers abruptly to the south near Basingstoke, heading insistently and noisily towards Southampton.

Within a gently undulating landscape and attractive rural hinterland, it is unfortunate that commercialisation and modern development have marred the historic and aesthetic appeal of the major towns and landscapes of northern Hampshire. Nevertheless, for those not rushing along its east–west axis or caught up in the daily grind of commuting, there is plenty of remaining unspoilt countryside to enjoy, together with a wealth of outdoor pursuits and some of the county's most impressive country houses.

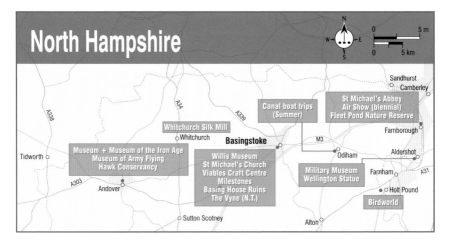

North Hampshire

N
W — E
S

0   5 m

0   5 km

Sandhurst
○ Camberley

A338

A34

A339

Canal boat trips
(Summer)

St Michael's Abbey
Air Show (biennial)
Fleet Pond Nature Reserve

Whitchurch Silk Mill
○ Whitchurch

Basingstoke
○

Farnborough
○

M3

M3   Odiham
○

Aldershot
○

Tidworth ○

Museum + Museum of the Iron Age
Museum of Army Flying
Hawk Conservancy

Willis Museum
St Michael's Church
Viables Craft Centre
Milestones
Basing House Ruins
The Vyne (N.T.)

Military Museum
Wellington Statue

Farnham ○

A31

A303

Andover ○

● ○ Holt Pound

Birdworld

○ Sutton Scotney

Alton ○

In the north-east corner of the county, **Farnborough** typifies the ribbon residential and commercial development that have characterised much of post-war planning in North Hampshire. According to the Guardian newspaper in 2007, the centre of Farnborough, with its uninspiring shopping precincts, was described as an 'abomination' by local councillors and the town itself as 'kind of dull'. This perception was based on an assessment of the systematic programme of heavy-handed demolition and development

Worth a Look

St Michael's Abbey

In 1871, the Emperor of the French, Napoléon III and his wife, Empress Eugenie, were deposed after the debacle of the Franco-Prussian War and were exiled to Chislehurst in Kent. After the death of the Emperor in 1873 and that of her only son, the Prince Imperial, in the Zulu War in 1879, the bereaved Eugenie decided to build a monastery that would serve as a home for monks expelled from France by the anti-clerical laws of the Third Republic and as a suitable mausoleum for her husband and son. In 1888, the bodies of Napoléon III and his son were moved to the Imperial Crypt at Saint Michael's Abbey, Farnborough, Hampshire, England. Eugenie, who died in 1920 was buried alongside them.

no historic buildings before the mid-Victorian era. The extensive heathland within which the town now stands was important in the Middle Ages for pasturage and two large ponds that produced industrial quantities of fish for the Bishops of Winchester. A document of 1491 mentions 'pike, tenches, perches, bream and roaches'. Fleet's current significance began in 1840 when the railway from London was completed and Fleet Pond station was built for the benefit of day-trippers. By 1860, there were 300 inhabitants, but no school until 1860 and no church until 1861. In 1878, property development led to the construction of a housing estate in the American style with roads arranged in a grid pattern. As in many parts of Britain, a building boom between the world wars led to sustained

Fleet (only) Best Bit

Owned and administered by the Army between 1854 and 1972, **Fleet Pond Local Nature Reserve** is located on the northern edge of the town, close to the station, and is an unexpected delight. The total reserve area of 57 hectares (141 acres) is designated a Local Nature Reserve. Within this, 48 hectares (118.5 acres) is designated a Site of Special Scientific Interest (SSSI). The Pond, at 21 hectares (52 acres), is Hampshire's largest freshwater lake and the circular walk, taking in both wet and dry woodlands, is strongly recommended. Details can be found at: www.fleetpondsociety.co.uk.

that has occurred since 1945, mainly to accommodate the constant pressure for housing, the spread of the commuter belt and a steep rise in business activity. Farnborough today is notable for the large number of technology and aerospace companies that have their main sites in and around the aerodrome, which is best known as the home of the Farnborough Air Show that takes place every two years. The town is also the international headquarters of BAE Systems, the multinational defence and technology giant.

Fleet is a dormitory and technology town that boasts very little heritage and growth and today the town is home to several business parks and Information Technology companies.

To the west, **Odiham**, whose name means 'wooded land' in Anglo-Saxon, was mentioned in the Domesday Book and was a significant settlement in the Middle Ages, sufficient to hold a 'parliament' in 1303 and, at one stage, having a population in Hampshire second only to Winchester. At its heart, it still preserves its medieval street plan, with the oldest section being designated a Conservation Area. Here, the attractive High Street contains a pleasant mix of Georgian and earlier, timber-framed buildings, many fronted with the brick so characteristic of the 18th century. Many people believe that Odiham, with its gentle, country town atmosphere, is the most visually appealing village in the whole of Hampshire. Its church is largely 14th-century Perpendicular, but with a large 17th-century tower. Inside are some interesting brasses and 17th-century fittings, including a pulpit and a funerary cart.

A short, pleasant walk along the canal brings one to the disappointingly sparse remains of **Odiham Castle**, which amount to a decidedly ruinous octagonal keep. Built by King John between 1207 and 1214, it was a powerful royal castle and provided a refuge for the king when he was besieged for 11 days by the French Dauphin (the future Louis VII), who had intervened on the side of the rebellious barons. After ownership by Simon de Montfort and use as a prison for King David II of Scotland by Edward III, the castle became derelict in the 15th century when it was used as a hunting lodge. It was described as a ruin in 1605 and the final coup de grace was delivered by the cutting of the canal through its outer walls.

Just to the south of Odiham is the Royal Air Force station of the same name, which is the home of the United Kingdom's force of Chinook helicopters, used for troop transport and heavy lifting. The helicopters, with their distinctive shape and twin rotors, can often be seen and heard flying around the local area.

To the south-east, **Crondall** is a picturesque village, with several appealing buildings, mainly clustered in The Borough and Church Street, and the faint traces of a Norman castle. The church is the familiar mix of Norman and Early English, but with an intrusive 17th-century brick tower, and there is a distinctive 14th-century brass.

Aldershot became a town in Victorian times after the expansion of the railways and the development of the Basingstoke Canal. Known as the 'Home of the British Army', the extensive 'Military Town' grew up from the 1850s as a major military garrison and training centre after 10,000 acres (4,000ha) were purchased in 1854 to provide a permanent encampment. The Victorian red-brick buildings and widespread service amenities still support and accommodate various units and elements of the modern Army and the area still has a decidedly 'military' feel.

Wellington Statue

Originally, this statue of the first Duke of Wellington on his horse Copenhagen was erected in 1846 at Hyde Park Corner on the Wellington Arch.

Best Bit

Military Museum

This agreeable specialist museum deals with the close relationship between the British Army and the towns of Aldershot and Farnborough over the past 160 years, as well as other aspects of associated local history. The collections contain an impressively large number of models, displays, uniforms, guns and vehicles, as well as a gallery devoted to the Canadian Army in Europe (whose base was in Aldershot during World War II). Most of the vehicles work and some are registered for road use, enabling them to travel to outside events. The museum has a regularly changing programme of events throughout the year and the Heavy Metal Thursdays in August (featuring armoured vehicles and weaponry) are justifiably popular.

Wellington Statue

However, it was not popular and Queen Victoria claimed that the statue ruined her view from Buckingham Palace. Finally, in 1885, it was moved to its present site – on Round Hill behind the Royal Garrison Church – after the Prince of Wales suggested (perhaps with tongue in cheek) that it be 'removed to Aldershot where it will be highly valued by the Army'. The massive statue is made from re-cycled bronze from cannons that were captured at the Battle of Waterloo and it took thirty men over three years to finish the project.

Further west, the prosperous village of **Hartley Wintney** is notable for its antique shops, its wide main street and a cricket pitch that claims to be the oldest continuously used ground in the world. The churchyard of St Mary's church (now redundant) holds the grave of Viscount Alanbrooke, the Chief of the Imperial General Staff during the Second World War and the primary military advisor to the Prime Minister, Winston Churchill.

Odiham Castle

Worth a Look (When You Can!)

West Green House

West Green House is an early 18th-century house owned by the National Trust, but let on a long lease to the present chatelaine, the noted garden designer, Marylyn Abbott. It has a series of attractive walled gardens, herbaceous borders and striking ornamental designs, including a kitchen garden and a grand water staircase.

Opening times are limited and visitors should check for details on www.westgreenhouse.co.uk.

Well to the north at the edge of the county, Sir William Pitt built Stratfield Saye House in about 1630. The house and estate were bought by the nation from the Pitt family in 1817 and presented to Arthur Wellesley, first Duke of Wellington, in recognition of his victory at the Battle of Waterloo. Still the home of the present Duke and Duchess of Wellington, the house contains many of the Iron Duke's personal belongings, his funeral carriage and an exhibition devoted to his life and times.

The Duke's old war-horse Copenhagen, which carried him the whole day at the Battle of Waterloo, is buried in the grounds of the house, next to an oak tree that grew from an acorn planted by a housekeeper at the time. The Duke himself has a monument in the grounds, which was erected in 1863 at a cost of £3,000.

The 550 acres (220ha) of parkland surrounding the house contain a country park that hosts a wide variety of activities, including nature trails, an adventure playground, a miniature railway and the National Dairy Museum, as well as a 35-acre (14ha) lake, with boating, fishing and windsurfing.

The medieval Church of St Mary the Virgin was demolished in about 1758 when the present church, also dedicated to St Mary, was being built, by George Pitt, first Lord Rivers. It is built of brick in the shape of a Greek cross and contains monuments to the Pitt and Wellesley families.

Surrounded by beautiful countryside and a patchwork of small villages, Basingstoke was at the intersection of several ancient routes in the Saxon period and was held by the king at the time of the Domesday Book. It became a prosperous market town in the Middle Ages and was a borough by 1622, with its wealth largely based on the cloth, malting and carrying trades. The expansion of rail and road links resulted in considerable commercial development in and around Basingstoke between the wars, followed by widespread suburban growth as part of the London Overspill plan. Basingstoke was rapidly developed in the late 1960s as an 'expanded town', with the population soaring from 17,000 in 1961 to 67,000 in 1981, and the town centre was completely rebuilt. Many buildings of historic interest (including a bomb-damaged Methodist church) were demolished to make way for a large red-brick shopping centre and a concrete multi-storey car park. Unsightly office blocks and large housing estates were constructed, as well as a ring road, which led to Basingstoke

Worth a Visit

Milestones

Milestones is an understated, thoroughly enjoyable 'living' history museum that displays and interprets the everyday artefacts, activities and preoccupations of people in Hampshire in the more recent past. Despite the initially unpromising approach through a retail park, an imaginative network of recreated streets is housed in an impressive modern building, within which visitors can wander at will. Two main Victorian and 1930s style streets include shops, houses and industrial buildings, as well as historic vehicles and people in period costume. In and around a succession of these themed exhibitions (for example, Taskers Works, a Fire Station and the Thornycroft Works), much of the social life of the 19th and 20th centuries is graphically presented in some depth.

All in all, the museum is decidedly family oriented, with an easy-going combination of generational recognition and nostalgia for adults and opportunities for participation and dressing-up for children. There are also regular themed exhibitions and events that will appeal to most visitors and a strong commitment to interpretation, supported by an interactive audio guide. The museum is an especially good choice for a rainy morning or afternoon. The visit could be combined with a visit to nearby Viables Craft Centre, in Harrow Way, where 14 independent businesses offer a range of distinctive art and craft goods in a semi-rural environment.

becoming known as 'Doughnut City' because of the rash of roundabouts.

Today, Basingstoke is a major residential and economic hub, with several major multinational companies, mostly from the communications, insurance and technology sectors, choosing to base their headquarters in or around the town, as well as light industry associated with IT, communications and pharmaceuticals. The 'Top of Town' and London Street contain most of what remains of Basingstoke's old town centre.

Separated from the hurly-burly of Basingstoke by the River Loddon, but still exposed to the noise of the nearby railway, **Basing** is an attractive red-brick village, with neat gardens and rural leanings, whose older houses were constructed with locally produced bricks and tiles. The parish church (St Mary's), of Norman origin, in brick with stone facings in the Perpendicular style of the late Middle Ages, contains Paulet family tombs. It required extensive restoration after being severely

Willis Museum

Started by a local archaeologist and watchmaker, the museum contains an extensive collection of watches and clocks, including a very rare Nuremberg clock-watch. In addition, there are various exhibits representing the social and economic history of Basingstoke and its local area, mainly dating from the early modern period. There are also other interesting displays on natural history, local archaeology and transport, including the Basingstoke Canal.

St Michael's Church

Somewhat out of place next to the shopping centre, this impressive church is a heavily restored, but striking Perpendicular building, probably dating from the 14th century, but with a mid-15th-century chancel and major additions and modifications in the early Tudor period. It also contains a Flemish painting of about 1539. During the successive sieges of Basing House in the Civil War, it was used as an explosive store by the Parliamentarians and suffered some damage. As a result of German bombing raids on the town, yet more damage was inflicted by the Luftwaffe.

Worth a Glance

The Chapel of the Holy Ghost (16th-century ruins), next to the Railway Station

Deane's Almshouse in London Street (1608)

All Saints Church (Victoria Street) – a remarkable example of a 20th-century (1915) foundation

knocked around in the Civil War.

Basing House is a splendidly evocative ruin that recalls a brutal and bloody siege during the English Civil War. Built in 1535, on the site of a medieval castle, this palatial residence, covering 8 acres (3.5ha), was the largest private house in the country, with around 360 rooms. During the First Civil War (1642–5), Basing was held for the king by the extremely wealthy Catholic magnate John Paulet, the 5th Marquess of Winchester and, over the space of three years, was a constant thorn in the side of Parliamentary commanders, both as a supply depot and as a secure base for raiding operations. Consequently, it was aggressively besieged by Parliamentary troops on three occasions, the last of which, at two years, was the longest of the war. In October 1645, when most of Charles I's field armies had been defeated, Oliver Cromwell arrived with heavy siege artillery and the house was violently stormed. Little quarter was given and the garrison was

Willis Museum, Basingstoke

Worth a Look

Despite its use by Parliamentary troops in the siege of Basing House and almost continuous use, a splendid late **medieval tithe barn** with a sympathetically restored roof is an unexpected treat.

largely put to the sword. Parliamentary troops pillaged the house and about £200,000 worth (about £24 million today) of goods were seized, before the building was destroyed by a fire accidentally started by the rampaging soldiers. Parliament ordered the complete demolition of the remains, giving licence to the local villagers to recycle the building materials.

The ruins have since been consolidated and recent excavations have revealed details of the house and its final days. As a result, the extensive site, with its huge medieval barn, charmingly restored 17th-century garden, picturesque ruins and exhibition make for an unexpectedly interesting and enjoyable visit for both adults and children.

The **Basingstoke Canal** was built between 1788 and 1794 and runs between Greywell (near Basingstoke) in Hampshire and Woodham in Surrey. It was designed originally to link London and Southampton and the Bristol Channel. However, it was never joined up with another canal and the route remained incomplete. Serving only Basingstoke when other projects were abandoned after World War I, it became uneconomical and fell into disuse. The subsequent collapse of the Greywell Tunnel in 1932 appeared to seal its fate, until restoration was undertaken by enthusiasts and the county councils of Hampshire and Surrey.

Today, the canal is 32 miles (52km) long, with 29 locks, and its status as a first-class leisure facility and Site of Special Scientific Interest (SSSI) is a tribute to the dedication and im-

Basingstoke Canal

agination of its restorers. The associated Basingstoke Canal Towpath Trail offers excellent walking on the flat (over 33.5 miles/54km), through varied countryside, with ample access points (especially from Odiham) and lots of opportunities for liquid and other refreshment on the way. Facilities for fishing and boating, mainly from Fleet and Odiham, are also available, as well as periodic narrow boat trips, mostly from the Colt Hill and Barley Mow bridges in Odiham.

The Canal Visitor Centre is at **Mychett**, just inside Surrey to the east of Farnborough, but boat and narrow boat trips are also available from Odiham from April to October.

One of best places to start a walk along the Basingstoke Canal is from **Crookham** village where the wharf has been converted into a car park.

To the North

North of Basingstoke, two features make **Pamber** worth a visit. Firstly the church, which comprises a massive Norman tower and an Early English choir, which were originally parts of a suppressed Benedictine priory, and secondly, the nature reserve in Pamber Forest, which, among its ancient oaks, is a haven for flowers and insects.

Also to the north is an exceptionally fine Tudor mansion, **The Vyne**, which was built between 1500 and 1520 for William Sandys, Henry VIII's Lord Chamberlain. After long occupation by the Chute family from the 17th century onwards, it was acquired by the National Trust in 1956. John Leland called it 'one of the principal houses in

Basing House ruins

goodly building in all Hamptonshire' and it has sustained its reputation into modern times. Within the house, there is an important and diverse collection of furniture, sculptures and paintings accumulated over the centuries, not least during a Grand Tour to Italy by John Chute in the 1740s. The house's compelling feature is its elegant Tudor chapel, with its brilliant Flemish stained glass, with portraits of Henry VIII, Catherine of Aragon and Margaret of Scotland, its intricately carved pews and canopies and Renaissance floor tiles.

With a classical portico added in the redesign of the building by the architect John Webb in the 17th century, the house sits in an exquisite location in a park that includes an ornamental lake and gardens. The park also has one of the earliest summerhouses in England and various woodland walks, as well as a wetlands area that supports a diversity of birds and other wildlife.

The Vyne is certainly worth a detour, but is subject to restricted opening times and potential visitors should check their plans in advance on www.nationaltrust.org.uk

The site of the Iron Age and Roman settlement of **Silchester**, known to the Romans as Calleva Atrebatum, lies roughly halfway between Basingstoke and Reading. Unlike most large Roman towns in Britain, it was completely abandoned after holding out for a considerable time against the invading Saxons in the early Dark Ages. Apart from its church and a single house, which was once a farm, the site is otherwise undeveloped and covered in fields. For the visitor, this is somewhat disappointing because all that can be seen above ground are the substantial remains of the Roman walls, built in the late third century and in places up to 13 feet (4m) high, and the earthworks of a first-century amphitheatre that used to hold between 4,500 and 8,000 spectators. The Museum of Reading, located in the Town Hall, displays many archeological finds from the various excavations at Silchester in a dedicated gallery.

Calleva is open to the public during daylight hours, seven days a week, and the full circumference of the walls is accessible, as is the amphitheatre. A circuit of the walls or a stroll across the site makes for a short, invigorating and thoughtful walk, while the Calleva Museum at Silchester Common has a number of visual displays. Visitors in the summer months are likely to see excavations by archaeologists and students from the University of Reading.

Another very appealing church is

Silchester Church

Near the former Roman east gate and possibly built on the site of a Roman temple is the parish church of Silchester, St Mary the Virgin, which dates from 1180 to 1200. Constructed with stones from the Roman town, it has largely escaped the restorative urges of the Victorians and is unusual because it has a long chancel and a relatively short nave. As well as a 14th-century tomb effigy and a noteworthy late-18th-century organ, it retains a 15th-century screen with flying angels, the remains of some 13th-century wall-paintings and a Jacobean pulpit of 1639.

at **Bramley**, three miles (5km) to the south. It has well-preserved wall-paintings, one of which (early 13th century) shows the murder of Thomas Becket and another (15th century) which is of St Christopher. Other features of interest are the gallery of 1728, late medieval stained glass (which was hidden in a nearby moat during Cromwell's time) and three interesting brasses. The Brocas chapel is worth a detailed look as well.

To the south of Basingstoke, on the road to Winchester, **Dummer**, whose name means 'the water by the hill', has a distinctive little church whose chancel dates from the early 13th century and which has several rare features. A gallery dominates the nave and the rood canopy is the only example that has survived in Hampshire. The church also contains a pulpit, dating from the

Wolverton Church

Also in the vicinity to the west, **Wolverton**'s red-brick church, built in 1717, is the best early Georgian church in the county. Despite its cruciform shape, a throwback to the Middle Ages unusual in the early 18th century, all the internal fittings are original, despite the windows, which were insensitively replaced in 1872.

late 14th century, which is one of only six in the country remaining from those times. The famous Wesleyan evangelist, George Whitfield, is known to have preached from this pulpit and, during his stay of six weeks, to have turned down the chance of a curacy in the parish.

Near Dummer, to the north-east, no true admirer of Jane Austen would miss a chance of a pilgrimage to **Steventon**, the place of her birth and where she lived until she was 25. Indeed, thousands arrive every year, although very little remains to be seen or directly experienced of her time there before she left for Bath. Born the youngest of seven children, with five elder brothers and one sister, Jane was the daughter of the rector at Steventon and nearby Deane. The parish was very much a family concern; after her father's tenure of 44 years, he was succeeded by her brother James and then her nephew, William Knight, remained in the post for 50 years. The rectory where she was born was demolished in 1826 and the only trace of it is a water pump in a field by the lane leading up to the church. The pump was probably outside the kitchen.

In St Nicholas' church, both the pulpit from which her father preached and the font in which she was christened have disappeared. There are, however, memorials to Jane and her brother James, who died in 1819, two years after Jane. Both James Austen and William Knight are buried in the churchyard and there is a sad memorial in the church to the latter's three daughters (aged 5, 4 and 3), who all died of scarlet fever in the same year.

Halfway to Andover, **Laverstoke** is an ideal place to appreciate the beauty of the upper Test Valley, which rises at Ashe and flows roughly southwards towards Southampton Water. The iron-free quality of the water here has long attracted paper manufacturers, particularly in recent times for banknotes. The paper-making industry began with Henri Portal, a Huguenot refugee, in 1712 at Bere Mill, a charming weather-boarded building between Laverstoke and Whitchurch. With success, he moved to Laverstoke and his firm won the contract to supply watermarked banknote paper to the Bank of England from 1724 until 1950. Production now takes place at De La Rue's modern facility at Overton Mill, alongside Overton Station.

Neighbouring **Whitchurch** was the first night stop for coaches out of London, allowing the crossing of the Test at the junction of two major roads. Situated on Frog Island on the river, Whitchurch has one of the last working silk mills in the country, built in 1815, with numerous silk fabrics and related goods for sale. The machinery is still in working order and visitors can see the restored looms and waterwheel in operation, or enjoy the very pleasant gift shop and tea room, which serves a variety of refreshments and light meals.

Andover had its origins in Saxon times, as Andeferas, and its medieval heart, before a disastrous fire in 1435, was near the church and priory. Its centre struggles to retain vestiges of its subsequent character as an 18th-century market town, where coaches to London, Southampton and Oxford used to stop. However, the remorseless spread of industry, several large Ministry of Defence establishments and various business enterprises in and around the town have swelled its population and diluted the quality and interest of its built environment. For those that like town trails, there is a collection of poems, set in granite or bronze, on a trail that starts from the Tourist Information Centre and takes in various works of public art along the River Anton. For Agatha Christie buffs, the site of the first murder in the The ABC Murders is Andover.

To the West

To the west, the county is dominated by a chalk ridge that gently slopes into Hampshire from Wiltshire, affording broad views and a distinctive pattern of settled rural life. Here, the countryside still seems somewhat detached from the rest of the county, but retains much of its overall character, with its chalk hills, deep winding lanes and views stretching into the distance. North of the A303, there is a great deal of unspoiled upland country, includ-

---

Best Bits

Andover Museum, in a former town house of about 1750, is a good example of an interesting, well-structured local collection, with thoughtful displays and exhibits about the history of the town and its area from the Neolithic period up to the present day. Natural History exhibits, together with examples of local fauna, fossils and habitats, complement the historic aspects to give a comprehensive impression of the local area.

The building is also home to the very worthwhile **Museum of the Iron Age**, which concentrates on daily life in the period from about 1500 BC up to the coming of the Romans. A wide range of representative artefacts is on display along with insights into life and occupations in the hill forts of the area from 600 BC (including finds from excavations at nearby Danebury Hill Fort).

Worth a Look

On its hill, **St Mary's** is possibly the finest and most intriguing Victorian church in Hampshire. Designed by the architect Augustus Livesay, the building was completed in 1846 in imitation of the Early English style.

The **Town Hall** of 1825.

Steventon Church

ing the highest point in Hampshire, Pilot Hill (at 938ft/286m), with quiet roads and communities whose roots are reflected in their ancient churches and field systems. The landscape is decidedly agricultural and open, with villages grouped closely together and extensive, sparsely occupied downland in between.

The Iron Age hill fort of **Danebury**, which has been systematically excavated and recorded using modern methods, is south-west of Andover. Surrounded by formidable earthwork defences, about 200 to 400 people lived here between 550 and 100 BC, at which point archaeology indicates that the fort, including its massive east gate, was destroyed by fire. Excavations have revealed almost every aspect of social life at the time, uncovering houses, pathways, temples and storage pits.

Also to the west, a nationally recognised, award-winning venture, **The Hawk Conservancy Trust** is set in 22 acres (9ha) of grounds that include woodlands and meadows. It is an unusually appealing attraction that combines conservation, education, rehabilitation and research. Visitors can see over 150 British and other birds of prey on show and there are three flying displays by birds of prey every day, themed around *Woodland Hawks & Owls*, *The World of Raptors* and *Valley of the Eagles*. All visitors are permitted to hold a British Bird of Prey, while special events include *Owls by Moonlight* and Adult and Junior Experience Days, which are designed to allow closer access to the birds. Children will be amused by the *Raptor Passport Trail* and a nature trail, but can also try ferret and runner duck racing. Detailed informa-

Andover Food Festival

Whitchurch Silk Mill

tion and timings of events are on www.hawk-conservancy.org.

Just off the A303, five miles (8km) west of Andover, is **Thruxton**, best known for its race track which lays claim to being Britain's fastest motor racing circuit. The track generally fields a wide variety of well-publicised and popular car, truck and motorbike events, including the British Super-bikes. The site also contains an airfield (formerly RAF Thruxton), which had a distinguished role in World War II, as home to various RAF aircraft and US Army Air Force P-47 Thunderbolts. It was civilianised in 1947. Thruxton village is largely unspoiled and, although the 13th-century church has been awkwardly restored, it has some interesting medieval effigies and tombs. Others will wish to note the White Horse, a 15th-century thatched pub at Mullens Pond, just south of the A303, and the George Inn, at the centre of the village.

Nether Wallop in Anglo-Saxon means the 'lower village in the valley of the stream' and the village heads off from a delightful mill house along a winding lane that is lined with brick and thatched cottages, while the road keeps to one side of the Wallop Brook. Across the brook is St Andrew's Church, which has 11th-century origins, but was successively extended between the 12th and 15th centuries. Among its important wall paintings, it has a 15th-century mural entitled *A Warning to Sabbath Breakers*, with a lurid representation of the wounds inflicted on Christ by the tools of those people who work on Sundays. There is also a rare brass, of Maria Gore, a prioress, commemorating her death in 1436, while outside is the unusual pyramid-shaped tomb of Sir Francis Douce.

In the past, Nether Wallop has been famous for the cricket bats made from local willow trees and owned by leading players such as W.G. Grace. The village is a good starting point for walks to the Iron Age hill forts at Danebury (2 miles/3km) and Woolbury Ring (5 miles/8km) and the River Test at Longstock.

The **Museum of Army Flying** at **Middle Wallop** has more than 35 aircraft on display, extensive dioramas and a number of imaginative displays. This national collection describes the growth of Army aviation from kites and balloons through to the Apache attack helicopter of today. It is located next to the main Army Air Corps training base, so visitors can usually see modern Army helicopters departing for training missions and exercises on Salisbury Plain. There is also a replica 1940s house, together with a cinema, a simulator, rifle ranges, and the usual range of refreshments and amenities. All in all, it is an interesting, engaging attraction for children of all ages, including adults!

West of the A34 and north of the A303, in an area known as the Hampshire Highlands, but properly as the North Hampshire Downs, the landscape is characterised by uninterrupted hill country and a maze of single-track roads. At its centre is a long chalk ridge, with breathtaking views in all directions, and, to the south, dozens of timeless, self-contained farming communities and extensive areas of ancient woodland.

Burghclere was once an important wool production centre for the blanket and cloth factories of Highclere and Newbury, as well as a source of lime for agricultural use, especially watercress. Now a pleasant residential village, some vestiges of its former life remain in the form of the abandoned lime-kilns and the watercress beds on streams leading down to the River Enborne.

At Burghclere, set amidst lawns and orchards, the red-brick Oratory of All Souls (**Sandham Memorial Chapel**) was built in 1923–6 as a memorial to Lieutenant H.W. Sandham, who died as a result of disease contracted while on active service in Macedonia during World War I. The chapel, influenced by Giotto's Arena Chapel in Padua, is remarkable for the English expressionist murals painted by Stanley Spencer between 1926 and 1932, reflecting the artist's own recollections, as a medical orderly and as an infantryman, of wartime military life in Macedonia.

Just south-east of the village on the edge of the north Hampshire Downs is the site of **Watership Down**, made famous by Richard Adams' 1972 novel. A pleasant method of approach on foot, with extensive views across to the Berkshire Downs, is along the Wayfarers' Walk from White Hill on the B3081 north of Overton. Also nearby are the unfinished earthworks of Ladle Hill, an imposingly sited Iron Age hill fort, which, with its incomplete ditches and spoil heaps, has revealed to archaeologists the techniques that were used in the construction of these earthworks.

Set in a magnificent park, mainly designed by Capability Brown and amid extensive lawns and gardens, **Highclere** is the stunningly impressive home of the Earl and Countess of Carnarvon.

Its present form has absorbed an older house that was completely rebuilt in the Elizabethan style by Sir Charles Barry between 1839 and 1842, incorporating Gothic, Moorish and Rococo interiors. The present building, the largest mansion in Hampshire, contains highly decorated effects, the desk and chair of Napoleon and collections of Old Master paintings. Most importantly, it has an outstanding collection of Egyptian treasures unearthed by the 5th Earl and his accomplice Howard Carter, both of whom are famous as the discoverers in 1922 of the tomb of Tutankhamun. Highclere will be familiar to many as the setting for numerous television and

Great View

A short distance away, the steep climb to the summit of the Iron Age fort of **Beacon Hill** is well worth the effort on account of the exceptional view in all directions. The hill fort has not been fully excavated, but the massive ramparts can be clearly seen. The grave of the 5th Earl of Carnarvon can be found on the site.

Just to the south and a short walk away, a memorial stone in the Seven Barrows field commemorates the day when Sir Geoffrey de Haviland (1882–1965), the pioneering aviator and designer, made his first successful flight on 10 September 1910.

There is a car park at the foot of Beacon Hill alongside the A34. On the way up, there is a step-way, but walking boots are generally needed after or during wet weather.

film productions, including *Jeeves and Wooster* and *The Secret Garden.*

Ashmansworth is interesting in its own right and a good place for walkers to base themselves. It has an attractive mixture of cottages and farm buildings, with lots of flint and thatch evident amid the brick and timber. The 12th-century church is largely unspoilt and while the Plough Inn can offer the highest 'pint' in Hampshire, Pilot Hill, the highest point in the county, is just over 2 miles (3km) away.

Just to the south, **Hurstbourne Tarrant** in its deep valley is known as 'Uphusband' in William Cobbett's Rural Rides and, with its buildings clustered around a small stream, is one of the prettiest in north Hampshire. Cobbett used to visit Joseph Blount, who lived at Rookery Farm House at the foot of Hurstbourne Hill, just to the south, where the front garden wall was known as the Wayfarers' Table, because

Danebury

Wherwell

Chilbolton

the farmer used to leave bread and bacon for passing travellers. He also kept a heavy horse to assist wagons up the hill. In one of the bricks of the garden wall, Cobbett has inscribed his initials, with the year 1825.

Just to the south of Andover, on the site of a demolished priory dating from the 10th century and a battle in 1141 in the Civil War between the forces of King Stephen and the Empress Mathilda, the highly attractive village of **Wherwell** contains a profusion of thatched, black and white timber-

Sandham Memorial Chapel

framed cottages. A 19th-century house called The Priory stands on the site of the abbey, founded in 986 by Queen Aelfrida to atone for the murder of her stepson, King Edward the Martyr, to ensure that her son Aethelred ('the Unready') would succeed to the throne. Some scattered remains of the abbey are in the grounds of the house. Elsewhere, the Old Malt House, Gaval Acre and Aldings are particularly appealing examples of the thatcher's art.

Museum of Army Flying

The pretty, compact church of St Peter and Holy Cross is 19th-century, although there are features remaining from an earlier building on the site, such as a 14th-century canopied tomb of a prioress and medieval sculpted faces that are built into the side of the Iremonger mausoleum. There is also a Tudor table tomb.

A bridge joins Wherwell and Chilbolton, by which walkers can access **Chilbolton Cow Common**, which is an area of open water meadows ideal for strolling and birdwatching with children. By the river, the Mayfly public house is a very welcome and enjoyable place to appreciate the surrounding countryside, although it is busy in the summer months.

Watership Down

Places to Visit

Aldershot Military Museum

Queens Avenue, Aldershot, GU11 2LG
☎ 0845 603 5635
www.hants.gov.uk/aldershot-museum
Open Mon–Sun 10am–5pm.

Andover Museum & Museum of the Iron Age

6 Church Close, Andover, SP10 1DP
☎ 0845 603 5635
www.hants.gov.uk/museum-of-the-ironage
Open Tue–Sat from 10am–5pm.
Admission free.

Basing House

Redbridge Lane, Old Basing RG24 8AE
☎ 0845 603 5635
www.hants.gov.uk/basing-house
Open Wed–Sun & Bank Holidays
2pm–6pm from Apr to Sept.

Danebury Hill Fort

Approx four miles north of Stockbridge
off the A30
www.hants.gov.uk/hampshire-
countryside/danebury
Open all day, every day. Admission free.

Highclere Castle

Highclere, Nr Newbury RG20 9RN
(Follow Brown tourist signs not sat-nav)
☎ 01635 253210
www.highclerecastle.co.uk
Open Sun–Thur from Jul and Aug
11am–4.30pm.

Milestones Museum

Leisure Park, Churchill Way West,
Basingstoke, RG22 6PG
☎ 0845 603 5635
www.hants.gov.uk/milestones
Open Tues–Fri from 10am–5pm, Sat &
Sun from 11am–5pm. Closed 25, 26
Dec & 1 Jan.

Museum of Army Flying

Middle Wallop, Nr Stockbridge
SO20 8DY
☎ 01264 784421
www.flying-museum.org.uk
Open daily 10am–4.30pm.

Sandham Memorial Chapel

Harts Lane, Burghclere, RG20 9JT
☎ 01635 278394
www.nationaltrust.org.uk
Open Apr to Sept, Wed–Sat from
11am–5pm; Oct from 11am–3pm; Mar,
Nov, Dec Sat & Sun from 11am–3pm.

Silchester Roman City

Near Tadley RG7 2
www.english-heritage.org.uk
www.silchester.rdg.ac.uk
Open daily all year. Admission free.

St Michael's Abbey

Farnborough GU14 7NQ
☎ 01252 546105
www.farnboroughabbey.org
Guided tour of the church and crypt
every Sat and Bank Holidays at 3pm.

Stratfield Saye House

Stratfield Saye RG7 2BZ
☎ 01256 882882
www.stratfield-saye.co.uk
Open Easter week and Jul 11.30am–
5pm Mon-Fri & 10.30am–5pm Sat–Sun.
Last entry to house at 3.30pm. Access
to house by guided tour.

The Hawk Conservancy Trust

Weyhill, Near Andover SP118DY
☎ 01264 773850
www.hawk-conservancy.org
Open daily mid Feb to Oct and Nov to
Feb from 11am–3pm.

The Willis Museum

Market Place Basingstoke RG21 7QD
☎ 0845 603 5635
www.hants.gov.uk/willis-museum
Open Mon–Fri 10am–5pm and Sat
10am–4pm. Admission free.

The Vyne

Sherborne St John Nr Basingstoke
RG24 9HL
☎ 01256 881337
www.nationaltrust.org.uk
Open mid March to Oct, Mon–Wed from
1pm–5pm and weekends from 11am–
5pm. Also open some dates in Dec.

Viables Craft Centre

The Harrow Way Basingstoke
RG22 4BJ
www.viablescraftcentre.co.uk
Open daily but times may vary.

Whitchurch Silk Mill

28 Winchester St Whitchurch RG28 7AL
☎ 01962 733810
www.whitchurchsilkmill.org.uk
Open all year (except Christmas/New
Year week) Tue–Sun from 10.30–5pm.
Open Bank Holiday Mondays.

GARDENS

The Vyne Gardens

Sherborne St John Nr Basingstoke
RG24 9HL
☎ 01256 881 337
www.nationaltrust.org.uk
Open weekends from Feb to Nov
11am–5pm. Also open some dates in
Dec.

The National Gardens Scheme

Visitors enjoy access to private gardens
which are not normally open to the
public and the money raised supports
a range of national and local charities.
Opening dates and times of the
gardens are available on the website:
www.ngs.org.uk. There are about 30
gardens which belong to the scheme in
North Hampshire.

COUNTRY PARKS

Yateley Country Park

Cricket Hill Lane Yateley GU46 6BB
☎ 01252 870425
www.hants.gov.uk/hampshire-
countryside/yateley-country-park
Open 24 hours, daily. Admission free.

2. Winchester and the Centre

The most genteel and ancient of Hampshire's towns and cities, **Winchester** is extremely well endowed with historical, archaeological and architectural features and has at its heart one of the most remarkable cathedrals in England, if not Europe.

Forever associated with Alfred the Great, the city is the burial place of an assortment (literally) of Anglo-Saxon and Anglo-Danish kings, together with William Rufus and a host of other worthies, including Jane Austen, Isaak Walton and William of Wykeham.

The earliest settlement appears to have been at St Catherine's Hill, to the east of the present city, where the earthworks of an Iron Age fort can be seen, along with extensive evidence of later occupation that has included use as a market and fair site and as a military mustering and defensive point. Today, a walk across the River Itchen and up to the hill gives a panoramic

Winchester Cathedral interior

Opposite Page: Winchester Cathedral*
*Left: Jane Austen's House

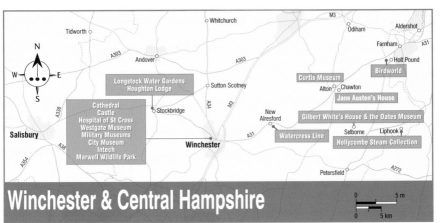

Winchester & Central Hampshire

0   5 m

0   5 km

view of the city and the surrounding chalk downs.

To the Romans, Winchester was *Venta Belgarum*, the administrative centre of the former British tribe of the Belgae and one of the two main Roman towns in Hampshire, along with Silchester (*Calleva Atrebatum*), the administrative centre of the Atrebates. It is noticeable that Winchester lies at the base of a system of roads that radiates to the west (to *Sorviodunum*, near Salisbury), to the north-west (to *Cunetio*, near Marlborough) and north-east (to Silchester), but not to the south. This suggests that the Roman system of trade and communication was integrated with the Thames Valley and that, until defence against Saxon and other raiders became a pressing issue, the heaths, swamps and forests of the south did not attract much attention. It was only towards the end of the 3rd century that the military fortifications of *Clausentum* (Bitterne, on Southampton Water) and *Portus Adurni* (Portchester) were

needed, to deter and repel military or raiding activity from that direction.

After the Romans, the archaeological and scanty historical evidence suggests that both Silchester and Winchester progressively decayed as trade declined and civic government weakened in the face of economic dislocation and increasing pressure from Germanic warbands and tribes. The most concerted

Winchester City Mill

pressure came from the north-east, from West Saxons asserting their hold over the upper Thames Valley and penetrating in force into northern Hampshire. It is likely that the civic authorities and community in and around Winchester held their own for some time, but, by 643, the town was a West Saxon possession and, as we learn from Bede, the bishopric was moved from Dorchester-on-Thames to Winchester in 676 to reflect this political shift.

From the time of the early West Saxon kings through to the Normans and before the rise of London as a political and commercial hub, Winchester was the effective administrative capital of England. With many of the instruments of government based there and with easy access for government and commerce, primarily to Normandy, through Portchester and Southampton Water, it was also one of the most important ecclesiastical centres of early medieval England. The medieval bishops of Winchester were powerful and exceptionally wealthy figures, with vast estates and revenues that rivalled or exceeded those of the leading secular noblemen. As a result, they expected, and were usually expected, to serve as expert administrators, dispense justice and hold high office as ministers and representatives of the Crown. Their wealth – and the assumption that in law, if not always in reality, they did not have family members who could inherit or benefit – also meant that they were able to invest time and resources in the city of Winchester and in building, agricultural and industrial projects within their wider diocese. Consequently, much of Hampshire's early, medieval development and historic remains reflect the considerable energies and resources of these immensely rich and intensely competitive medieval personalities who combined the roles of chief executives and prelates.

After the medieval period, Winchester's trade and importance declined as Southampton and other towns gained the advantage. However, by the time of the Napoleonic Wars, it had recovered much of its prosperity and eminence as a centre for local administrative and agricultural activity. By the 19th century and with the coming of the railways, it was a significant garrison and supply depot, acting as the hub of Hampshire's financial services and agricultural products, as well as developing a fashionable social scene for the local gentry.

Along with most other historic cities, the centre struggles to maintain its dignity and distance amid the pace of modern commerce, the demands of tourism and of an impatient consumer society. However, by and large, retail and housing development has been sympathetically kept at bay and the survival of individually owned shops has helped maintain a more traditional atmosphere at the heart of the city. Also, the outline of Winchester's past is reflected faithfully in a street pattern which has changed little since the major replanning and rebuilding of the 9th century – and within a city centre circuit that has remained unchanged since Roman times.

Therefore, visitors, if they wish to make the best of their time in Winchester, are strongly encouraged to view the sights and move around the city on foot. Almost all the major historical features and attractions are readily accessible and the experience is likely to be infinitely more rewarding as a result.

Winchester Cathedral

The choice of site for the longest cathedral in Europe, at 556 feet (170m), in the midst of what must have been distinctly watery meadows and unstable ground, seems on first viewing to be an odd one. However, the original 7th-century building was probably constructed of wood and, its position would have been almost at the centre of what had been the Roman city, must have reflected the power of tradition. This cathedral, enlarged, rebuilt in stone and extended over three centuries, was superseded by a massive structure in 974–94 that was probably the largest church in England at the time. Its major attraction was the shrine of St Swithun and it was the prestigious venue for coronations and the burials of kings, including Alfred and Cnut. With a diocese that stretched from the Thames to the Isle of Wight, the Old Minster and its precincts were the focus of a large ecclesiastical and royal quarter of the city, which had itself been extensively refounded as a new town in the late 9th century. The foundations of this Old Minster can be seen on the ground to the north side of today's cathedral. Also within the ecclesiastical complex was the New Minster, built in 901–3 and which served as the parish church until moved to nearby Hyde in 1100, and the Nunnaminster (nuns' minster), founded by Alfred in the late 9th century.

The present cathedral of St Swithun was started by Bishop Walkelin in 1079 and consecrated in 1093, although the tower dates from 1110, after its predecessor collapsed in 1107. It was at the time the longest cathedral in the Christian world and today is only exceeded by St Peter's in Rome. It is 556ft (179m) long, 217ft (66m) broad at the transepts and 109ft (33m) to the roof line, with the tower extending to 138ft (42m). Norman work survives in the crypt, the transepts and the core of the nave. Successive additions, renovations and extensions occurred over the centuries, notably under Bishop de Lucy (1189–1204), in extending and remodelling the choir and crypt in the Early English style, as well as adding a Lady Chapel; Bishop Edington (1346–66), in taking forward the rebuilding of the choir and restoring the decayed Norman west front and nave in the Perpendicular style; and Bishop William of Wykeham (1367–1404), in continuing this work, adding the nave aisles and embellishing the Norman nave pillars (completed by Bishops Beaufort and Waynflete in the 15th century). The choir stalls, with their vigorously carved misericords, date from 1295–1310 and Bishop Fox (1500–38) commissioned the great East Window – still, miraculously with its original glass – and the side-screens of the choir. The wonder is that Henry of Blois, the most hyperactive builder-bishop of Winchester in the 12th century, did not feel the urge to contribute.

There is so much of interest in the cathedral that it would be pointless and tiresome to give an exhaustive inventory of all those features and

Right: Winchester High Street
Above: Winchesters café
Below: The Round Table

monuments that will naturally attract attention. Visitors will be able to stroll around this historical and ecclesiastical treasure house at leisure and guidebooks of varying depth and detail are available on site. However, the following features should not be missed:

● In the north aisle of the nave is the plain, unadorned memorial to Jane Austen, with the more expansive stained glass window of 1900 above it.

● Nearby is an outstanding example of the distinctive black Norman Tournai fonts, of which there are four in Hampshire (out of seven in Britain). In intricately carved detail, this one tells the story of St Nicholas of Myra, the patron saint of children and seafarers.

● Next, there are ornate chantry chapels to Bishop Edington (1366, in Purbeck marble) and the great William of Wykeham (1404, in the more flamboyant Perpendicular style).

● Under the tower, by the north transept, the Chapel of the Holy Sepulchre (early 13th century) has exceptional wall-paintings depicting *The Entry into Jerusalem, The Descent of Christ from the Cross and Burial and Doubting Thomas.*

● The 'Compleat Angler', Isaak Walton, who died in 1683, is buried in the Silkstede Chapel in the south transept, with a memorial window above. The wooden oak benches are probably 12th-century and the Pilgrim Gates are wrought iron from the early 13th century.

● The distinctive tomb in the floor of the chancel is thought to be that of King William II (Rufus), who was killed while hunting in the New Forest in 1100.

● The choir contains beautiful early 14th-century carved choir stalls, complete with their canopies.

● The side-screens in the choir supposedly hold the bones of various West

Saxon and Danish kings (named on the chests). The skeletons were scattered by Parliamentarian troops in the Civil War and it is doubtful whether the bones were re-assembled as precisely as 'it says on the box'.

● The reredos behind the altar was built in the 15th century, but its original statues were destroyed during the iconoclastic reign of Edward VI and replaced in the 19th century.

● Behind the altar are the remains of two Tudor chantry chapels – of Bishops Fox (1528) and Gardiner (1555) – built in the nick of time before the whole idea of chantry chapels was swept away by the Reformation.

● The modern shrine of St Swithun, built in 1962, to replace the one destroyed in 1538 in the reign of Henry VIII, is in the retrochoir. Originally buried outside the Old Minister, the saint's bones were brought inside in 971 and a stone outside the current cathedral marks the site of his grave. In the retrochoir, it is also worth noting the most extensive area of medieval floor tiles in England and two further chantry chapels – Bishops Waynflete (1486, with an intricate vault) and Beaufort (1447, but with a 17th-century replacement effigy).

● The bronze memorial here to William Walker recalls the prodigious feat of a diver who between 1906 and 1912 underpinned the whole east end of the cathedral with concrete to prevent its collapse. Working underwater, alone in the dark and with the constant danger of being buried alive, he excavated a huge volume of muddy soil and manhandled tons of aggregate and concrete into position.

● The late 12th-century Lady Chapel was extended to celebrate the christening of Henry VIII's elder brother Arthur in 1486 and the reproduction wall-paintings cover the much faded and threatened originals underneath. Earlier wall-paintings can be seen in the Guardian Angels' Chapel.

● The Norman crypt is only accessible in the summer months because of the threat (tellingly) of flooding. The eastern crypt dates from 1189 to 1204.

● The Cathedral library – containing thousands of rare books and manuscripts – dates from 1150. Its world-famous exhibit is the elaborately – though incompletely – illuminated Winchester Bible, which was written and illustrated from about 1160.

● Examples of early stonework and statuary can be found in the Triforium Gallery, while the Treasury holds an exhibition of ecclesiastical silver and other plate.

The south side of the cathedral is the site of the old cloister and St Swithun's Priory. Its demolition in the reign of Elizabeth necessitated the construction of the large flying buttresses, so that this side of the cathedral would not collapse. Now part of the Close, the Prior's Hall still stands, next to the Deanery, together with the earliest known hammer-beam roof in England in the 13th century Pilgrims' Hall. Beyond St Swithun's Gate is King's Gate, one of the two remaining of the medieval town gates. Unusually, this gate has the church of St Swithun in its upper storey, built originally to provide for the spiritual needs of the laity who were working in the priory and the adjacent ecclesiastical establishments.

A stroll through King's Gate brings the visitor to College Street (on the left). Jane Austen died at Number 8 in 1817 after moving from Chawton the year before so that she could have ready access to medical advice and treatment.

Winchester College

Winchester has justifiable claims to be the oldest public school in the country and its extensive presence and grounds dominate the streets and area to the south of the cathedral close outside Kingsgate. The school was founded for 70 poor and needy scholars to study classics and grammar in 1382 by Bishop William of Wykeham, a local Hampshire boy made good, and pupils of the school are consequently known as Wykehamists. The original medieval buildings of 1387–93 have been modified or extended over the centuries, with the significant additions of 'School' in 1687, with its menacing inscription advising pupils to 'learn, leave or be licked', a War Cloister, to commemorate the Wykehamists who were killed in the two world wars, and New Hall, which was completed in 1960. The 1395 chapel, with its tower, was restored in the 19th century, but retains the very fine ceiling and upper vault constructed by the same group of craftsmen who built Westminster Hall roof.

Wolvesey Castle

The fortified residence of the Bishops of Winchester was built in the 12th century in the south-eastern corner of the city, largely by Henry of Blois, the bishop of Winchester between 1129 and 1171. His residence originally consisted of a large hall block (the 'west hall'), begun by his predecessor, to which he added another hall block (the 'east hall') with over 40 rooms, and then, as civil war threatened, a keep, a defensive circuit of walls and two gatehouses. The castle was continuously occupied and modified over the subsequent centuries, but, having been the venue for Queen Mary and Philip II of Spain's wedding reception, was severely damaged and partly dismantled during the Civil War. Next door is the surviving wing of the Bishops' Palace built by Thomas Fitch in 1684, but largely demolished in 1786. As the Bishop's House, the west wing is the home of today's bishop and incorporates a Tudor chapel that used to be part of the castle.

From College Walk, a walk of about a mile will take the visitor along a pleasant footpath and across the water meadows of the River Itchen to the Hospital of St Cross (less active folk can retrace their steps through the Close and approach the Hospital by car or bus on the long way round along St Cross Road).

The Hospital of St Cross

Founded by Bishop Henry of Blois in 1136, the Hospital of St Cross is the oldest continuously operating charitable foundation in England and its range of medieval buildings, almshouses and seemingly over-endowed, but exquisite Norman church remind visitors of the support and hospitality available to medieval pilgrims and travellers. The Hospital itself was founded to support thirteen poor men and to feed one hundred men each day.

Today, this quietly impressive institution is home to the Master and Brethren of St Cross – who are distinguished by their traditional black gowns, trencher hats and Maltese Cross badges – and offers a unique insight into age-old customs of hospitality and community care. Also sharing the site is the Order of Noble Poverty, which was founded in 1445–6 by Cardinal Henry Beaufort, when he rebuilt the hospital and added 35 'distressed gentlefolk' to the list of pensioners. These Brothers today wear claret robes, claret trencher hats and silver cardinals' badges. St Cross has places for 25 Brothers in total, each of whom has a self-contained flat on the ground or first floor of the buildings dating back to the 15th century.

Visitors are able to wander around the various medieval and Tudor buildings, most of which date from the Beaufort rebuilding of 1446, and which include the Brethren's Hall, the cloisters and the church, as well as the charming gardens. They can even request the Wayfarer's Dole (a small beaker of beer and a morsel of bread), although most would probably prefer, during summer months, the refreshments available in the 'Hundred Men's Hall', built on the site where, in the past, the hundred 'deserving' poor men received their daily ration.

The church, dating from 1170 to 1230, is probably one of the best examples of the Transitional style (Norman to Early English) of architecture in the country. Norman features, such as the font and nave aisles, are mixed up with pointed arches and windows and the whole building, with its restored tower of 1386 and the complications induced by a 19th-century restoration, is a pleasant confusion of Norman power and Early English elegance. For visitors who like to work things out, it is well worth (and fun) dwelling on the detail.

Winchester Castle

The strategic importance of Winchester, and its subsequent development as the administrative and military headquarters of the Anglo-Norman and Angevin empire, led to the construction of a castle as early as 1067. It was greatly extended and strengthened under Henry III, who added a series of strong defensive works and the Great Hall, and by Edward I. Unfortunately, little trace remains today of this most powerful of the royal castles of medieval England, apart from the Great Hall itself and a short section of foundations.

This is because the castle, along with the city, was held for Charles I during the Civil War and, after its capture by Oliver Cromwell and Sir William Waller, Parliament ordered its demolition in 1646. The site was later acquired by Charles II (for five shillings!) in order to construct the King's House, a palace designed by Sir Christopher Wren and supposedly inspired by Versailles. This imposing building, abandoned by James II in 1688, was never used as a palace and between 1796 and 1894 it was used as a refugee centre and as a military barracks. Following a major conflagration which destroyed the King's House in

St Cross Hospital

1894, the Peninsula Barracks were built, which incorporated the central colonnade of Wren's building around a large parade ground. The barracks have more recently been converted into elegant apartments and houses.

However, the famous Great Hall, spared by the Parliamentarians, who considered it useful for council meetings and assizes, is the main reason for making the effort to visit the site. Erected between 1222 and 1235 of local flint with Purbeck stone dressings, the Hall, built with an interior 110ft by 55ft by 55ft (34m x 17m x 17m) in a double cube design, originally had lower walls and a roof with dormer windows. In the 14th century, the roof was replaced and the dormers were removed, resulting in the remodelling of the building and the insertion of the tall fan-traced windows. The Hall was extensively restored in the 1870s, when the entrance was altered and moved to its present position, and was last used as a court between 1938 and 1974.

Inside hangs a huge wooden Round Table, long reputed to be that of King Arthur, but, in reality, of 14th-century origin and construction. Some 18 feet (5.4m) in diameter and weighing around 1.2 tons (1,200kg), it was re-painted in its present form during the reign of Henry VIII in order to impress the Holy Roman Emperor during his visit to Winchester. The table has the names of 24 of Arthur's knights carefully inscribed around its edge.

Just outside the south door of the Great Hall is a re-creation of a medieval herbarium in honour of Eleanor of Provence, wife of Henry III, and her daughter-in-law Eleanor of Castile, wife of Edward I. It was opened in 1986 by HRH The Queen Mother as part of the 900th anniversary of the Domesday Book. Nearby, the excavated remains of part of the castle's foundations, including a round tower, a garderobe and a sally port, can also be seen.

The Great Hall

Westgate Museum

A short walk leads to the Westgate and its small museum, at the upper end of the High Street and dominating the city. The Westgate, which was built in the 12th century and extended in the 13th and 14th centuries, is one of only two surviving fortified medieval gateways in the city and has a portcullis and two early gun ports. After the medieval period, it saw service as a gaol and debtors' prison, as graffiti carved by prisoners in the upper chamber can testify. Its museum features displays themed around Winchester history, especially the medieval period. Arms and armour are on display, together with everyday artefacts and a painted ceiling created for the marriage of Mary I to Philip of Spain in 1554. Brass-rubbing experiences are also available, while children can try on armour.

Military Museums

The **Guardroom Museum** at the 19th-century Peninsula Barracks serves as a visitor centre for all the museums on site and, with a wealth of artefacts and archives, brings to life the social and organisational aspects of Army life over the past 400 years.

The Rifles Museum, incorporating the collections of two recently merged regiments (the Light Infantry and the Royal Green Jackets), offers an outstanding collection of uniforms, weapons, regimental silver, paintings and medals, together with 34 of the (new) Regiment's 59 Victoria Crosses, and a detailed diorama of Waterloo, comprising over 22,000 model figures.

The **Gurkha Museum** displays the distinctive contribution made by the Gurkhas since their adoption by the British Army in 1815 and their unwavering courage in all the campaigns fought by the British up to the present day. Other exhibits portray the way of life in Nepal and describe notable incidents in Gurkha military history.

At **Horsepower**, the Museum of the King's Royal Hussars describes the history and fighting culture of three famous cavalry regiments (the King's Royal Hussars, the Royal Hussars (Prince of Wales's Own) and the 14th/20th King's Hussars), as well as telling the story of the Charge of the Light Brigade during the Crimean War.

A short walk away at Serle's House in Southgate Street is the **Museum of the Royal Hampshire Regiment**, which has in recent years been absorbed into the Princess of Wales's Royal Regiment. With models, paintings and other interesting military paraphernalia, the Museum gives an insight into the life and history of the regular, militia and volunteer elements of a county regiment that had seen continuous service at home and abroad since its formation in 1702.

The City Museum

The City Museum is in The Square, just off the Cathedral Close. Well-planned and presented, it tells the story of Winchester from prehistoric times up to the present day in a series of exhibitions that are easy on the eye and full of interesting curios. A representative sample of artefacts, coins and mosaics combines with reconstructed Victorian and 20th-century re-creations to get the balance about right, with hands-on activities and quizzes for children.

High Street

The old Guildhall has a locally made bracket clock, which activates a curfew bell at 8 pm every night, in honour of a tradition stretching back to Norman times. Opposite is God Begot House, supposedly on the site of a house owned by Emma, queen of King Cnut, and The Royal Oak, which claims the oldest bar in England. Further along is the High Cross, known as the Butter Cross because of its site as a market and dating from the Middle Ages. Just behind, the entrance to St Lawrence's church can be found, on the site of a Norman palace or royal chapel. Here, every new bishop is presented to the mayor and citizens before processing to the cathedral and his enthronement.

Worth a Glance

St John the Baptist

On St John's Street, St John's Church is a rare survival of an unrestored Early English parish church, with arcades and pillars dating from the late 12th century and fragments of 13th-century wall paintings.

Hyde Abbey

Represented only by its 15th-century gatehouse today, Hyde Abbey was founded in 889, but re-established in its present form in 1110 to accommodate the monks and royal tombs from the New Minster. As such, it was the final burial place of many of the late Anglo-Saxon kings, including King Alfred. Unfortunately for pilgrims seeking out places associated with Alfred, Hyde was dissolved and demolished under Henry VIII; later building works on the site in 1787 disturbed a number of coffins and it is likely that the royal bones are all now dispersed.

Passing by the City Museum, High Street appropriately widens into the Broadway, where the Victorian Guildhall and the defiant statue of Alfred the Great can be found. The monument, designed by Hamo Thornycroft, was erected in 1901 to commemorate the 1,000th anniversary of the death of the king, which is odd, because Alfred died in 899! A myth of uncertain origin claims that if a female virgin of at least 16 years old walks around the statue three times in a clockwise direction, Alfred will lower his sword.

A little further on, beyond the site of the demolished East gate, the passage over the river marked the eastern boundary of the city and the area over the Itchen was known as the Soke. The City Mill, by the bridge, was rebuilt in 1744, and is in the care of the National Trust.

Near Winchester

Originally an Iron Age earthwork, which also contained a number of prehistoric and Saxon burials, **Oliver's Battery** seems to have been used as an encampment or artillery park for the Parliamentary forces besieging the city in 1645. It is unlikely to have been a 'battery' as the range of the cannon at that time meant that they were not able to fire their projectiles as far as the city. However, the guns could have been used to block approaches by Royalist relieving troops.

INTECH is a lively, interactive, hands-on experience, which seeks to educate and stimulate interest in the fields of science, technology, engineering and mathematics (STEM). It is housed in an impressive 35,000 square foot (3,500 sq m) purpose-built building at Morn Hill and consists of over 100 exhibits, which demonstrate the fundamentals of science and technology in an accessible and entertaining way. There is a dynamic programme of exhibitions and demonstrations, as well as a leading-edge digital planetarium, which seats 176 visitors at any one time.

Winchester High Street

took the name of the village as part of his title when he was ennobled.

To the West

The parish church of **Sparsholt**, St Stephen's, contains sections ranging from the 12th to 19th century in age. The parish also contains the small hamlet of Dean, Farley Mount Country Park and Crab Wood SSSI. The grounds of the 17th-century Lainston House (now a hotel) contain the ruins of the 12th-century St Peter's Church. Archaeological discoveries have included Bronze Age bowl and disc barrows. Sparsholt College, a leading college for land-based industries, is located on the outskirts of the village.

Farley Mount Country Park is a Site of Special Scientific Interest (SSSI), a large expanse of woodland and downland where there are plenty of opportunities for walking and admiring the landscape. A Roman road, with its distinctive raised causeway, can be seen in West Wood near the site of a Roman villa, whose mosaic is in Winchester City Museum. The pyramid on Farley Mount recalls a horse that fell into a chalk pit with its rider and both sur-

To the North

Sutton Scotney is notable for having been the site of numerous Spitfire crashes in the Second World War. It has a population of more than 200, and had a watercress-based economy. Its best-known resident was J. Arthur Rank, the industrialist and film producer, who

Avington Church

Between Winchester and Alresford, Avington has possibly the finest Georgian church in Hampshire (Wolverton is a very close second), dating from 1768 to 1771. Happily unrestored, its visually impressive mahogany fittings, with their careful craftsmanship and sense of proportion, are made from wood said to have come from a Spanish ship captured as a prize. Particularly noteworthy are the squire's pew, the domed pulpit and the coved plaster ceiling, together with the gallery and its barrel organ. The church was built by Margaret, Marchioness of Carnarvon, whose tomb is on the north side of the altar.

The Watercress Line

The 'Alton, Alresford and Winchester Railway' was established by an Act of Parliament in 1865 and, as the Mid-Hants Railway, opened four years later. The Mid-Hants line was closed in 1973, but was partially re-opened in 1977, as the Watercress Line (it used to transport fresh watercress). This restored steam railway now runs between New Alresford and Alton, where it connects

with the mainline service to London. This recalls the fact that Alton used to be an important railway junction, linking the Mid-Hants Railway with the Meon Valley Railway which ran to Fareham between 1903 and 1955. Another line also used to run northwards to Basingstoke.

The **Watercress Line** is now the name of the Mid-Hants Railway, which runs for 10 miles (16km) from New Alresford to Alton, with intermediate stations at Ropley and Medstead & Four Marks. At Alton, it is connected to the national rail network. The line was purchased from British Rail in November 1975 after the line had been closed in 1973. The line was reconstructed and opened in stages between 1977 and 1985. Structures and equipment were acquired from other stations and railway companies, together with a range of steam and diesel locomotives and rolling stock. As with any Heritage Railway, there is a heavy emphasis on authenticity and the stations and infrastructure are lovingly restored. Nostalgia firmly rules here, with a variety of steam and other specials, as well as themed 'Thomas the Tank Engine' trains, with thinly disguised locomotives. There are refreshments and a play area (at Ropley), picnic areas (at Alresford and Ropley) and gift shops (at Alresford, Ropley and Alton).

vived unhurt. The horse was renamed 'Beware Chalk Pit'.

To the East

The pretty village of **Avington** is situated in a very picturesque, wooded part of the Itchen valley. The manor occupied by **Avington Park** used to belong to the cathedral of Winchester, until it was granted by Henry VIII to Edmund Clerke. By the middle of the 17th century, George Brydges, a courtier and official of Charles II, had acquired the estate and began to expand the accommodation to incorporate beautifully gilded and decorated formal rooms, such as the Hall, Ballroom, Drawing Room and Library. Outside, the striking red-brick house has a visually impressive classical portico and extensive gardens that include a lake, two rare iron conservatories and an orangery.

Pronounced 'Allsford', **New Alresford** is never called 'new' by locals, even though the adjoining village is called Old Alresford! Alresford was a borough in Saxon times, prosperous because of its corn, wool and farming produce. Its prosperity increased when, in 1190, the Bishop of Winchester drained the marsh where the Alre, Sutton and Bighton streams met, to form a 200 acre (80ha) dam and made the river navigable all the way to Southampton Water. Its remains – a 60 acre (25ha) pond – is a haven for water birds and the arch of the 14th-century Great Weir still links Old and New Alresford. The town has also thrived with its traditional trademark industry – the growing of watercress.

Successive fires between the 12th and 18th centuries destroyed many of Alresford's buildings and the architectural character of the town, not least the deliberate firing by the Royalists after the Battle of Cheriton in 1644. Despite modern accretions, it still has a distinctly 18th-century character, although behind the facades brick and timber and wattle and daub constructions can still be found. Broad Street remains particularly attractive and there are plenty of traditional shops, craft and design outlets and tea rooms.

To the north of Alresford, near Northington, **The Grange** is set in a splendid situation that commands sweeping views. The core of the house was built between 1665 and 1673, but after it was acquired by Henry Drummond in 1787 the Grange was completely redesigned by William Wilkins and rebuilt between 1809 and 1816 in the classical Greek style. Unfortunately, although it was a sensation in its day, Drummond lost interest in the project and the conversion was never fully completed. By 1970 it had been reduced to an empty shell. However, an extensive restoration programme has allowed the repair and preservation of the building, which remains empty. Visitors can walk around the building and view the landscaped grounds. Features worthy of note are the 17th-century west front and the portico on the east front which was based on the temple of Theseus in Athens, as well as a glass and cast-iron conservatory, erected in 1824, which has an Ionic portico.

Just to the south, the pretty village of **Tichborne** is well known for two historical associations. The first is the story of the Tichborne Dole, a yearly provision for the poor of a gallon of flour started by Roger de Tichborne in 1150 at the request of his dying wife. The parsimonious Roger said that he would grant an amount of flour equivalent to the yield of an area around which his wife, Mabel, could walk holding a flaming torch. Mabel struggled around a circuit enclosing 23 acres (9 hectares) and, before dying, promptly pronounced a curse that would see a generation of Tichborne sons followed by one of solely daughters, thus ending the line, if the grant were revoked. This actually occurred in 1794, when magistrates stopped the dole and the grant had to be quickly re-introduced to prevent a family crisis

Worth a Look

The church at Tichborne is Saxon in origin, but, despite obvious surviving Saxon and Norman features, such as the chancel and some arcading, is mainly 14th century and later medieval, with a great deal of late Tudor and Jacobean woodwork. The brick tower dates from 1703. Curiously, the north aisle, behind the iron railing, is the preserve of the Tichborne family, who remained attached to the Roman Catholic faith after the Reformation and who contrived to continue their worship here in the subsequent centuries. Their monuments are to be found in the church, notably the fine Jacobean memorial to Sir Benjamin Tichborne.

that was subsequently averted.

The second association is the case of the 'Tichborne Claimant', an infamous example of identity theft in the 19th century. Roger Tichborne was presumed to have been lost at sea, but, after many years, Arthur Orton, a butcher from Australia arrived to claim his inheritance. He was a plausible claimant, but his case was eventually thrown out in one of the longest trials in English legal history and he was convicted of perjury.

A little further south, the neo-Tudor house of **Hinton Ampner** is built on the site of a Tudor house that was demolished in 1793 and has at its heart a late-Georgian building, which was subsequently refashioned and expanded. However, from 1935, much of the additional building was demolished and the gardens redesigned in an attempt to recreate an 18th-century effect. The house required further consolidation and restoration after a catastrophic fire in 1960, but, among other treasures, retains its fine collection of Regency furniture and Italian paintings.

The gardens themselves are very easy on the eye and well known for their clever designs and subtle combinations of formal and informal settings, backed up by immaculate lawns and imaginative topiary. Beyond, there are uninterrupted views of the Hampshire countryside.

North-east of the village is the battlefield of **Cheriton**, where the Parliamentary forces of Sir William Waller defeated a Royalist army in March 1644. This victory opened the way for the capture of Winchester by Parliament and the collapse of King Charles I's

Alresford

military position in southern England. A 5½ mile (8.7km) walking trail around the battlefield has been established, which passes places that were significant on the day of the battle. It is supported by a Cheriton Battlefield Walk leaflet, which describes the route and provides a commentary on the battle. The leaflet is available through the tourist information centre on ☎ 01962 840 500 or via tourism@winchester.gov.uk.

Further east on the Farnham road, with its clearly defined, mature High Street and market square, **Alton** has a population of about 17,000. Recorded occupation dates from Roman times, when a posting station and settlement was established at Neatham, close to a ford crossing the River Wey. An early Saxon settlement – 'Aewielltun' (the settlement at the river source) – grew up and excavations at a large seventh-century cemetery have revealed a range of grave goods, including the Alton Buckle which is on display in the Curtis Museum. The Danes defeated a Hampshire army here again in 1001, but, by the time of the Domesday Book, 'Aoltone' was a thriving market town, with evidence of considerable trading activity. The Treaty of Alton of 1101 settled the crown on Henry I, after he came to terms with his elder brother, Robert, Duke of Normandy.

Throughout the Middle Ages, Alton, sitting astride the major routes from London to Winchester, Southampton and the New Forest, was well known for its fairs and markets, as well as the bands of robbers who operated in the Pass of Alton. The traditional fairs continued well into the Victorian period. Records for the 18th century reveal a cheese fair taking place alongside the stalls of tinkers and local people, selling lace, gloves, books, gingerbread, bodices, sugar plums, knick-knacks and household goods. By the late Victorian period, fairs tended to deal mainly in horses, sheep and agricultural products, mainly hops and barley. Alton also developed a thriving local industrial base

built around brewing, and there have been breweries in Alton since 1763. Today, the multinational Coors Brewing has a brewery in Alton which produces Carling, Grolsch and Worthington at the Manor Park Brewery. Other industries once included the manufacture of paper and haberdashers' materials.

During the English Civil War, a small Royalist force was quartered in the town when they were surprised by a Parliamentary army of around 5,000

Above & top:
Jane Austen's House at Chawton

Sweet Fanny Adams

On 24 August 1867, an eight-year-old girl, **Fanny Adams**, was murdered and horrifically dismembered by Frederick Baker, a local solicitor's clerk, who became one of the last criminals to be executed in public at Winchester. One of the public notices advertising his execution is in the Crown public house and Fanny Adams' grave can still be seen in Alton cemetery. The notorious murder occurred at the same time as the introduction of tinned meat in the Royal Navy. This innovation was disliked by the sailors, who quickly claimed that tins contained the remains of 'Sweet Fanny Adams' or 'Sweet F.A.'. This has led to the expression which today is a euphemism for 'absolutely nothing'.

men in December 1643. The Royalist cavalry fled from the town, leaving Colonel Richard Boles and the infantry to fight it out. They refused to surrender and retreated to St Lawrence Church, where Boles was killed with 80 of his men and over 700 Royalist soldiers were captured in the final assault. Evidence of the battle and the bullet holes can be seen in the church, especially in the oak south door.

The **Curtis Museum** was founded in 1856 by Dr William Curtis and now houses an excellent local and social history collection. It contains prehistoric artefacts, Roman pottery reconstruction, Saxon burial goods, mementoes from the Battle of Alton of 1643, together with a particularly well-researched and presented exhibition of the local life and associations of Jane Austen. It also has themes dealing with the story of Fanny Adams and various local industries and pursuits.

Its outstanding exhibit is the highly ornate Alton Buckle, found in the Mount Pleasant Anglo-Saxon cemetery in the grave of a sixth- or seventh-century warrior with a sword, shield boss and spear heads. Another eye-catching object is the uniquely enamelled bronze Selborne Cup, which was found amid a large number of Roman artefacts and second-century coins on the site of Blackmoor House in Woolmer Forest.

In 1809, Jane Austen moved to **Chawton**, to a cottage that was part of her brother's estate, and lived there for most of the last eight years of her life, a time when she published *Sense and Sensibility* and *Pride and Prejudice* and produced *Emma*, *Mansfield Park* and *Persuasion*. Her house, about which she wrote that 'when complete, it would all other houses beat', is now a thriving museum and quiet study centre, with many personal items directly associated with her life and work, including furniture, books and manuscripts.

The garden has been restored, as far as possible, to its original condition and two oak trees on the road outside were planted by Jane on her arrival at Chawton. The donkey cart used by the author for her trips into Alton can still be seen in the bakehouse.

The family connection with Chawton arose when Jane's brother, Edward, was adopted by his cousin, Thomas Knight, who owned the Chawton estate, and inherited the nearby 16th- and 17th-century manor house. He had, however, to change his name to Knight to inherit the estate. A more famous brother, Francis, was an admiral of the fleet, who, as captain of the *Canopus*, had narrowly and (for him) frustratingly missed the Battle of Trafalgar in 1805 because he had been temporarily detached by Nelson for convoy duty in the Straits of Gibraltar. He is thought to have been the model for the character of William Price in *Mansfield Park*. Jane's younger brother Charles was also prominent in the Royal Navy and became a rear admiral.

Owing to the progressive onset of what was possibly Addison's disease or Hodgkins' lymphoma and the need for constant medical attention, Jane Austen spent the last two months of her life in Winchester and was buried in the north aisle of the cathedral in 1817, aged 41.

To the South-East

Five miles south-east of Winchester, **Marwell Wildlife** is a 140-acre (55ha) landscaped park that is home to over 200 unusual and endangered species and represents the cultural move away from the traditional zoo. Centred on Marwell Hall, a medieval timber-framed cruck house which underwent a major rebuild in 1816, the park has always been committed to breeding rare animals and species at risk of extinction, such as Asian lions, snow leopards and scimitar-horned oryxes. It attempts to combine conservation and research with meaningful public access, through the use of imaginative ways of allowing visitors, especially children, close yet unobtrusive views of the animals. The animals are largely grouped in environmentally themed areas and so one is able to see giraffes, zebras and ostriches happily mingling in the *African Valley* section, while there are the usual antipodean suspects, wallabies and kookaburras, in the *Australian Bush Walk*. Especially imaginative are the ways in which a 30ft (10m) walkway allows eye contact with the giraffes and an underwater feature gives a clear view of swimming penguins. *Tropical World* completes the themed environments.

As one would expect, there are numerous opportunities and venues to take refreshment and relax amid the wildlife (notably at the *Café Graze*), as well as a Science and Learning Centre for the serious-minded. There is also a road-train that transports visitors around the site, stopping at designated intervals and taking about 30 minutes for the round trip. Keepers and staff are on hand at various times in the day to talk about their charges and their habitats.

Halfway between Winchester and

Bishop's Waltham Palace Ruins

Portsmouth, and meaning 'the bishop's settlement in the forest', **Bishop's Waltham** was well established in Saxon times at the head of the River Hamble, but was destroyed by the Danes in 1001 AD. By 1086, it had a substantial population of about 300 and belonged to the Bishop of Winchester. In 1136, Bishop Henry of Blois, the brother of King Stephen, built a fortified palace, extended and improved by William of Wykeham in the 14th century, which survived intact until the Civil War, when it was dismantled. Its substantial ruins remain and the site is well worth a visit, as is its Norman church.

Its historic prosperity in future generations is reflected in its many Georgian houses, and by the 19th century Bishop's Waltham was a thriving market town, with several agricultural enterprises, a cattle market and a large brickworks. Today it retains much of its former elegance and is noted for its individual shops and close connection with the surrounding agricultural community.

Giant Ant Eater, Marwell Wildlife

Places to Visit

Avington Park

Near Winchester, SO21 1DB
☎ 01962 779260
www.avingtonpark.co.uk
Open May to Sept on Sun and Bank
Holidays only and Mon in August from
2.30pm–5.30pm.

The Allen Gallery, Alton

Church St, Alton, GU34 2BW
☎ 0845 6035635
www.hants.gov/museum/allen-gallery
Open Tue–Sat 10am–5pm. Admission
free.

The Curtis Museum, Alton

High St, Alton, GU34 1BA
☎ 01420 82802
www.hants.gov.uk/curtis-museum
Open Tues–Sat 10am–5pm. Admission
free.

Bishop's Waltham Palace

Bishop's Waltham, SO32 1DH
☎ 01489 892460
www.english-heritage.org.uk
Grounds open May–Sept 10am–5pm
every day except Sat. Admission
free. Farmhouse with exhibition open
weekends only. May to Sept 2pm–4pm.

Hinton Ampner

Bramdean, nr Alresford, SO24 0LA
☎ 01962 771305
www.nationaltrust.org.uk
Open mid Mar to Oct, Sat–Wed
11.30am–5pm, restricted weekend
opening in Dec.

Jane Austen's House

Chawton, Nr Alton, GU34 1SD
☎01420 83262
www.jane-austens-house-museum.org.uk
Open daily Mar to Dec from

Jane Austen's House

10am–4.30pm (5pm Jun–Aug) Open
weekends Jan & Feb 10am–4.30pm.
Closed 25 & 26 Dec.

Marwell Wildlife

Colden Common, SO21 1JH
☎ 01962 777407
www.marwell.org.uk
Open daily (except 25 & 26 Dec) from
10am–5pm. (closes 6pm mid-Jul & Aug
& 4pm Nov & Dec).

Northington Grange

Northington, Nr Alresford, SO24 9TG
☎01424 775705
www.english-heritage.org.uk
Open daily all year 10am–4pm

City Mill

Bridge St, Winchester, SO23 0EJ
☎ 01962 870057
www.nationaltrust.org.uk
Open Wed–Sun 11am–5pm (4pm in
winter) and Bank Holiday Mon plus
some Mon & Tues.

The City Museum

The Square, Winchester, SO23 9EX
☎ 01962 863 064
www.winchester.gov.uk
Free admission. Open Apr to Oct: Mon–
Sat 10am to 5pm, Sun 12pm–5pm,
Nov to Mar: Tues–Sat 10am–4pm, Sun
12pm–4pm.

Places to Visit

The Great Hall

The Castle, Winchester, SO23 8PJ
☎ 01962 846476
www.hants.gov.uk/greathall
Open daily 10am–5pm. Occasional
closures for civic event. Admission free.

Hospital of St Cross

St Cross Road, Winchester, SO23 9SD
☎ 01962 851375
www.stcrosshospital.co.uk
Open daily from Apr to Oct 9.30am–
5pm; 1pm–5pm on Sun; Nov to Mar
10.30am–3.30pm from Mon–Sat only.

Intech Science Centre & Planetarium

Telegraph Hill, Morn Hill, Winchester,
SO21 1HZ
☎ 01962 863791
www.intech.co.uk
Open daily from 10am–4pm.

Westgate Museum

High St, Winchester, SO23 9JX
☎ 01962 869864
www.winchester.gov.uk
Open from Apr to Oct daily 10am–5pm
(12–5pm on Sun) & from Feb to March
Tues–Sun 10am–4pm (12–4pm on
Sun). Admission free.

Winchester Cathedral

The Close, Winchester, SO23 9LS
☎ 01962 857200
www.winchester-cathedral.org.uk
Open daily from 8.30am–6pm (5.30pm
on Sun). For entrance fee check
website. No admission fee for those
attending services or praying privately.

Winchester College

College Street, SO23 9NA
☎ 01962 621 209
www.wincoll.ac.uk (see college &
community – guided tours)
Guided tours take place throughout the
week but are subject to change.

Wolvesey Castle

College St, Winchester, SO23 9NA
www.english-heritage.org.uk
Open every day from Apr to Oct 10am–
5pm. Admission free.

Winchester Military Museums

Peninsula Barracks, Romsey Road,
Winchester, SO23 8TS
☎ 01962 828 541
www.winchestermilitarymuseums.co.uk

The Adjutant General's Corps @ the Guardroom

☎ 01962 877826
www.armymuseums.org.uk
Open Tues–Sat 10am–5pm. Sun 12–
4pm. Admission free.

The Rifles Museum (including the Royal Green Jackets Museum)

☎ 01962 828549
www.rgjmuseum.co.uk
Open Mon–Sat 10am–5pm.

The Gurkha Museum

☎ 01962 843 659
www.thegurkhamuseum.co.uk
Open Mon–Sat 10am–5pm Sun 12–
4pm. Closed 25 & 26 Dec, 1 Jan.

Horsepower

☎ 01962 828541
www.horsepowermuseum.co.uk
Open Tues–Fri 10am–12.45pm &

1.30–4pm Weekends & Bank Holidays 12–4pm. Admission free.

Royal Hampshire Regiment Museum

Serle's House, Southgate Street, SO23 9EG
☎ 01962 863658
www.royalhampshireregimentmuseum.co.uk
Open Apr to Oct from 10am–4pm and Bank Holidays 12–4pm. Admission free.

The Watercress Line

The Railway Station, Alresford, SO24 9JG
☎ 01962 733810
www.watercressline.co.uk
For train times please check website. Stations at Alresford, Ropley, Medstead & Four Marks & Alton.

GARDENS

Hinton Ampner Gardens

Bramdean, nr Alresford, SO24 0LA
☎ 01962 771305
www.nationaltrust.org.uk
Open mid Mar to Oct, Sat–Wed 11am–5pm; restricted weekend opening in Dec. For entrance prices check website.

Queen Eleanor's Gardens Winchester

The Castle, Winchester, SO23 8PJ
☎ 01962 846476
www.hants.gov.uk/greathall/eleanor
Open daily 10am–5pm. Admission free.

The National Gardens Scheme

Visitors enjoy access to private gardens which are not normally open to the public and the money raised supports a range of national and local charities. Opening dates and times of the gardens are available on the website: www.ngs.org.uk

COUNTRY PARKS

Farley Mount Country Park

SO22 5QS
☎ 01962 860948
www.hants.gov.uk/hampshire-countryside/fmcp
Open 24 hours, every day. Admission free.

Despite being watered by the rivers Itchen and Test, the strip of land running from east to west across the neck of Southampton Water is densely urbanised and contains not only one of the busiest ports in Europe, but also the major concentration of Hampshire's motorway and railway networks.

As a result, much of the area, especially that to the north towards Eastleigh and the regional airport, is dominated by technological, residential and commercial development, while to the east, Portsmouth and Southampton, despite the mutual antagonism of their citizens, both appear destined to merge as one vast conurbation at some stage. However, to the west, more open countryside and the water meadows of the upper Test Valley present a more appealing prospect, as do the distinctive charm and variety of the New Forest.

Situated on the peninsula formed by the confluence of the Test and the

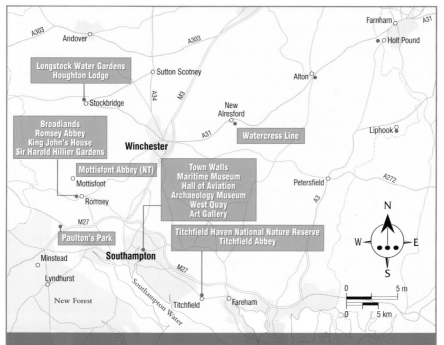

Andover
A303
A303
Farnham
A31
Holt Pound

Longstock Water Gardens
Houghton Lodge

Sutton Scotney

Alton

Stockbridge

New
Alresford

A34
M3

Broadlands
Romsey Abbey
King John's House
Sir Harold Hillier Gardens

Winchester

A31

Watercress Line

Liphook

Mottisfont Abbey (NT)

Mottisfont

Town Walls
Maritime Museum
Hall of Aviation
Archaeology Museum
West Quay
Art Gallery

Petersfield

A272

Romsey

A3

M27

N

Paulton's Park

Titchfield Haven National Nature Reserve
Titchfield Abbey

W   E

Minstead

Southampton

S

Lyndhurst

M27

New Forest

Southampton Water

Titchfield

Fareham

0   5 m

0   5 km

Southampton, Romsey & the Test Valley

Itchen ('Test is west') and possessing a deep-water natural roadstead, **Southampton** is by area Hampshire's largest city and one of Europe's largest, busiest commercial ports. As a result of town planning that seems to have been dictated by the urgent need to recover from German bombing in World War II, Southampton – with its uninspiring, widely dispersed centre and extensive suburban sprawl – is not a visually attractive city. A great many people pass through, either on their way to one of the huge cruise liners based or departing at the port or to a ferry to the Isle of Wight. Even more, thanks to the M27 and M3 motorway combination that skirts the city, pass by altogether en route to the West Country or the nearby New Forest.

However, the evocative reminders of its seafaring tradition, its dominant position on Southampton Water and a convenient mix of modern amenities and historic features provide the visitor with a range of enjoyable possibilities and memorable experiences. The circuit of its medieval city walls contains some of the best-preserved remains of their type in the country and the city amply repays the effort of exploration on foot. The shopping centre has the full range of high street shops, several department stores and the usual amenities. Major new developments are designed to make Southampton the leading retail and shopping centre on the south coast.

The area covered by modern Southampton has been settled for an extremely long time and evidence for prehistoric activity is scattered all over the city. The earliest finds associated with human activity date from the Stone Age, and Bronze Age objects have surfaced regularly. Similarly, Iron Age earthworks have been identified at Lordswood and Aldermoor, together with salt workings and pottery at other sites in the area. Iron Age buildings have been excavated, together with a variety of artefacts, in the city centre.

A Roman settlement was established at Bitterne soon after the conquest of AD 43 on a promontory on the east side of the River Itchen, a mile to the north of the medieval town. Probably known as Clausentum, it became a thriving port and military depot and excavations have uncovered the remains of a bath-house, warehouses, roadways and tracks, as well as defensive banks and walls. The base seems to have been abandoned early in the fifth century, although evidence suggests that the defences were re-used in the ninth and tenth centuries.

The Saxon settlement grew up on the opposite bank of the Itchen in what is now the St Mary's area of the city and became one of the largest towns in Anglo-Saxon England, known as variously as *Hamwic* or *Hamtun*. Excavations on various sites, especially in the Six Dials district, have revealed an extensive range of Saxon artefacts, confirming that the town was one of the more important trading emporiums in Europe. Its size and importance, as well as a population of four to eight thousand, probably explain why the county came to be called *Hamtunscir* and then *Hantescire* in the Domesday Book.

Hamwic seems to have declined around the time of King Alfred and after, possibly because of the growth of Winchester as a rival market, but more likely because of the disruption and loss of its international trade caused by constant Viking raiding. By the tenth century the settlement was again fortified and, following the Norman Conquest in 1066, Southampton became the major port of transit between London, Winchester and Normandy. The castle was built in the 12th century and by the 13th century Southampton had become a leading commercial port, primarily trading in Bordeaux wines and English cloth and wool. The surviving remains of its 12th-century merchants' houses testify to its wealth at this time.

Two major disasters struck the city in the 14th century. In 1338 it was attacked, sacked and burned by a French and Genoese fleet and in 1348–9 the population was depleted by possibly half by the arrival of the Black Death in England. As a result of the raid of 1338 and the increasing use of the town for cross-Channel military campaigns, the fortifications were significantly reinforced and extended. The city walls ran for 1¼ miles (2km) and surrounded the peninsula between the mouths of the Itchen and the Test, with a moat cutting off the fourth side to the north.

Most of the building seems to have taken place in the periods from 1260 to 1290 and 1321 to 1382, with continuous improvements made into the 15th century, including God's House Tower, built in 1417, which was the first purpose-built artillery fortification in England. The walls later became superfluous once the extensive – and expensive – system of artillery forts was constructed under Henry VIII in the 1540s along Southampton Water and around the Solent.

By Tudor times, the town was heavily involved in trade with the Mediterranean and Venice, but its commerce suffered as competitors, such as Bristol and the West Country ports, exploited new routes to India and the Americas. Hit badly again by the plague in the 1660s, the town and its trade stagnated, before recovering in a new role, that of marine spa and health resort, based on sea-bathing. Its status was enhanced by a visit from the Prince of Wales in 1750 and various facilities were built, such as assembly rooms and a theatre. Jane Austen lived in a house in Castle Square between 1806 and 1809.

However, its importance was significantly revived by the military and transportation demands of the Napoleonic Wars. The Industrial Revolution, the development of steam-powered ships and the arrival of the railway saw Southampton transformed into a major port of commerce and embarkation, supporting not only Britain's imperial ventures and wars, but also supplying and trading with her overseas territories. High levels of emigration to parts of the Empire added to the load on the port and, during the 19th century, the

docks developed on a vast scale, to the extent that Southampton became the main point of embarkation for the Boer War and the First World War and associations began with famous shipping lines, such as Cunard, Union Castle, White Star and the Peninsular and Oriental Steam Navigation Company (P&O). During the interwar period, there was yet another massive expansion of the docks, mainly on reclaimed land to the west. They consequently suffered heavy bombing by the Luftwaffe in World War II, notably in the winter of 1940–1.

Modern Southampton has adjusted

The Double High Tide

An odd Solent phenomenon is its double high tide, which was so distinct as to be mentioned in Bede's *History of the English Church and People* in the eighth century. The first tide comes straight up the English Channel through the Needles Channel from the west and produces the first high water. Two hours later, another tide, which started out in the Atlantic about 12 hours before the first one, and flogged its way around the top of Scotland and through the Dover Strait, arrives from the east. Just as the (first) tide is starting to ebb, it returns to a high tide again (with the second), before ebbing rapidly to complete the cycle. This has given the Solent distinctive tidal features and considerable problems for the unwary, careless navigator or sporting sailor

West Quay Shopping Centre

to the realities of 21st-century globalisation and its economy is centred on retail, light industry, tourism and a greatly re-profiled maritime enterprise, based around cruise liner, container and automobile freight and ferry traffic.

The Town Walls – Few towns in Britain have such considerable remains of their defensive architecture still standing and much of the western circuit has been preserved from German bombing and the malign attentions of council officials. There is an excellent series of signs at key points explaining

Fountain outside the City Art Gallery and Central Library

The Town Walls

the history and significance of various features and a walkway along the length of the walls. Guided tours are available through the Tourist Office.

The **Bargate** is one of the best-preserved medieval town gatehouses in the country, with its original Norman arch dating from about 1170–80, two late-13th-century drum towers and a striking 15th-century forebuilding. The room on its upper floor was a guild hall until 1938 and the building has also been used for collecting tolls, as a prison and as a museum. In former times, trams had to be specially fitted with domed roofs to pass through the archway. In a niche on the restored south side is a statue of George III in the guise of a Roman Emperor.

Outside the Bargate, Richard, Earl of Cambridge, Henry Scrope, 3rd Baron Scrope of Masham and Sir Thomas Grey of Heton were executed in 1415 just before King Henry V's departure for France on the expedition that led to the Battle of Agincourt. These ring-leaders of the so-called 'Southampton Plot' had been summarily tried at what is now the Red Lion public house in the High Street.

The walls to the west of Bargate predominantly date from the period after the French raid of 1338. The north-west corner of the town was secured by the Arundel Tower, which leads to the best-preserved section of the walls as they run south towards the Catchcold Tower, with its novel gun-ports. Before

One of Southampton's many parks

Worth a Look

At the south end of the arcades, the **Norman House** (also known as King John's Palace) is one of the earliest 12th-century houses in the county, with two storeys, characteristic windows and a fireplace, as well as 14th-century gun-ports.

Next to West Gate, the **Tudor Merchant's Hall** used to be in St Michael's Square and was a fish market and clothier's hall. It was moved to its present position in 1634, to serve as a warehouse.

Just beyond West Gate is the Mayflower Memorial, commemorating the sailing of the Pilgrim Fathers in 1620, on the *Mayflower* and the *Speedwell*, together with the **Stella Memorial**, to Mary Ann Rogers, a stewardess who sacrificed her life in a shipwreck.

At this point, there is the **Mayflower Park** opposite, the **Royal Pier** built in 1833 and on the corner of Bugle Street, the former **Yacht Club** of 1846. Also on the corner of Bugle Street, as the wall bends to the southeast and becomes ruinous, is the **Wool House**, a medieval storehouse, with cylindrical buttresses, that was built and owned by the abbey of Beaulieu. Once used to house Spanish prisoners of war, it is now the **Maritime Museum**.

Town Quay, which used to be the commercial and shipbuilding hub of medieval Southampton, is now a modern development that contains ferry terminals, offices and a yacht marina.

---

the land was reclaimed to the west, the sea used to lap against the wall all along this western wall and one shortly comes to the Water Gate of the castle that used to stand on the inside of the walls at this point. The castle, which was of the motte-and-bailey variety, was demolished in 1818 and the mound lowered. The next section of wall, with its arcading, probably represents some of the strengthening that occurred after the raid of 1338 and there are numerous apertures through which missiles could be dropped on would-be assailants. Passing the Blue Anchor Postern and the Norman House, the next major feature is the West Gate, which used to give access to West Quay, the only berth suitable for large ships in the medieval period, from which Henry V in 1415 and the Pilgrim Fathers in 1620 departed.

In the **Maritime Museum**, there is an extensive and rewarding collection of items relating to Southampton's maritime heritage, including scale models of liners and other ships, a lot about the story of the Southampton-based Titanic and its crew, many of whom were local, and a fascinating model of the docks. Just further on from the Wool House is the so-called **Canute's Palace**, a 12th-century Norman upper-hall house and at the end of the High Street are the remains of five other houses and the old town Water Gate, which was demolished in 1806, although one of its towers can be seen in the Castle Hotel. In Winkle Street is the 12th-century St Julian's Chapel (normally closed), where the 'Southampton Plot' conspirators were buried and, at the south-east corner of the town walls, God's House Gate and Tower.

God's House Tower was built in the late 14th or early 15th century and is one of the earliest custom-built artillery fortifications in Europe. The ground floor was an armaments store and the upper story a gun battery, which was used to repel a French attack in 1459. It is now the **Archaeology Museum** and it contains a well-ordered, attractively presented exhibition of the history and archaeology of Southampton, with particularly interesting exhibits from the Roman and Dark Age periods, as well as an Egyptian collection of Sir Flinders Petrie.

Nearby, God's House Green, first used in 1299, could possibly be the oldest bowling green in England.

From here, the medieval walls used to head north and there are few traces for the visitor to see until one reaches the Polymond Tower, at the north-east corner of the town. More vestiges can be seen on the track of the northern wall on the way back to Bargate. Only the connoisseur will find the effort worthwhile.

Other Highlights

St Michael's Church

Founded in about 1070 and the only survivor of five medieval churches in the town, it is probably the oldest build-ing in Southampton, although only the base of the tower is original Norman. It was considerably expanded between the 12th and the 15th centuries with the addition of aisles, arcades and side chapels, to the point where the original cruciform shape has disappeared. It was also much altered and modified in 1828. However, it does have some interesting features, including one of the four black marble Tournai fonts in Hampshire, with symbols of three of the evangelists, Matthew, Mark and John, and some grotesques, as well as chained copies of Foxe's Book of Martyrs and a two-volume Commentary on the Bible. The tomb of Sir Richard Lyster commemorates a Lord Chief Justice who died in 1552 and who used to own the Tudor House opposite the church. Finally, there are two fine 14th- and 15th-century lecterns.

Tudor House Museum

This Tudor town house, with its large hall, was restored in 1911 and is currently undergoing another major refurbishment programme. Dating from 1495 it once hosted Henry VIII and Anne Boleyn on a visit to the town. To the rear is a reconstruction, with authentic materials and objects, of a Tudor garden. The Norman house, King John's Palace, can be accessed through the garden.

Southampton Hall of Aviation (Solent Sky)

Situated on Albert Road South, on the way to Ocean Village, this wonderful museum is an unusually absorbing collection of aircraft that have been important in the aviation history of the local area, including some impressive naval jet aircraft and some iconic names, such as the Tiger Moth, the Spitfire and the Sea Vixen. There is also a wealth of information on every aspect of the development of aviation in the 20th century, with a major emphasis on R.J. Mitchell, the designer of the Spitfire fighter, and his Supermarine factory in Southampton, where the Spitfire was first built and tested.

Medieval Merchant's House

In French Street is a shop and house dating from 1290, furnished in the style of the medieval period.

Ocean Village

Ocean Village is on the River Itchen about half a mile to the east of the city. Located in the former Princess Alexandra Dock, it is a large marina and residential development that houses multiplex cinemas, cafés and restaurants.

West Quay

This large city centre shopping complex has more than 90 shops on three levels. With one of the best selection of shops

God's House

Maritime Museum

on the South Coast including a large John Lewis there is ample parking. Open every day from 9am–7pm except Sundays 11am–5pm.

Civic Centre Art Gallery

The Civic Centre is home to a police station, the council offices, an entertainment venue, the city library and the art gallery. The award-winning gallery houses an important and enjoyable collection of over 2,800 items. With a wide span of exhibits, it has French impressionists, a variety of European works from the 17th and 18th centuries and 20th-century British paintings, as well as numerous assorted sculptures and ceramics.

To the West

Some people will wish to make the pilgrimage to **East Wellow** church to visit the grave of Florence Nightingale, who lived at nearby Embley Park both when she was a child and when she died, aged 90, in 1910. Her burial place is marked by an obelisk, which, although recording in full the names of her family, simply recalls the great nursing innovator as 'F.N.'. The 13th-century church has interesting features, such as Jacobean furnishings, but its once-graphic medieval wall paintings depicting various saints are now very fragmentary and faded.

As the visitor moves west, there is a perceptible change in the topography, with the urban and tarmac-dominated landscapes giving way to the distinctively well-watered and fertile countryside of the Test Valley. Along the river valley itself is a succession of picturesque villages and market towns, which seem to blend naturally into the background, together with a range of very attractive views, especially in spring and summer.

Probably Hampshire's most appealing market town, **Romsey**'s obvious attractions are its remarkable ancient abbey church and the nearby **Broadlands** estate, once the country seat of the politically (and personally) irrepressible Lord Palmerston, who was born there, and now the home of the Mountbatten family. Nevertheless, as another of Hampshire's prosperous, elegant market towns that manages to retain its balance and character amid the pressures of modern life, it fully repays an exploration of its shops and streets.

The town probably owes its existence and subsequent growth to the establishment of the nunnery by Edward the Elder in 907 for his daughter Ethelflaeda, who became its first abbess, and the present Market Place probably stands on the site of its Saxon and medieval ancestors. The abbey was refounded by King Edgar as a Benedictine nunnery in 967, but in about 993 it was captured by the Danes and the nuns were dispersed.

Probably revived during the reign of Cnut, it was distinguished enough for Christine, the sister of the last Saxon prince, Edgar Aetheling, to be abbess. Her niece, Maud, entered the nunnery, but was induced to marry Henry I and is known to history as Queen Mathilda. King Stephen's daughter, Mary, was abbess in 1160 and this continuous royal patronage probably accounts for the extensive building of the 12th century and the flourishing of the town.

The abbey's later history followed the general pattern of English medieval life, with periodic visitations from the plague, noble patrons and the bishops of Winchester, who discovered various scandals from time to time among those whose vocation had perhaps slipped or among the high-born ladies for whom the abbey was intended as a retreat or a retirement home. The abbey was finally dissolved in 1538, when the abbess and 25 professed nuns were pensioned off and the church was sold to the townspeople for £100.

Romsey's medieval wealth was gained primarily from the production of wool and almost certainly milling, given the numerous streams and the River Test flowing through the town. It received a charter from James I in 1607 and by the 18th century was famous for its brewing and agricultural produce. In the Victorian era, its prosperity was assured by the coming of the railway and the prestige derived from its close proximity to the denizens of Broadlands.

The Abbey

Without question (in our opinion) one of the best churches in Hampshire and possibly the finest Norman building in the country (Durham Cathedral runs it close), the present structure was probably begun – or progressed – by that prolific Hampshire builder and bishop, Henry of Blois, at some stage in the 1120s and 1130s. The remains of part of its Saxon predecessor, with its distinctive apse and possibly dating from the reign of Edgar or Cnut, have been excavated and are on view today. The interior is a delicate combination of predominantly Norman and Early English architecture. Dating from about 1120 to 1150, the choir, transepts and tower are the earliest features, along with the initial building of the nave up to the third bay. Subsequent resumption of work from the last quarter of the 12th century, in the Early English period, saw the completion of the last three bays in the first quarter of the 13th century, as well as replacement of the Norman windows at the eastern end of the church, beyond the altar. In passing it is worth noting that the Norman triforium arches in the three most easterly bays of the nave and in the choir and the transepts, with the gap between the upper and subsidiary arches filled only by a single pillar, are architecturally unique.

The altar itself has a carved relief of the Madonna and Child, while in the north transept is a painted early Tudor reredos showing the Resurrection of Christ and a group of saints. Its preservation occurred simply because, after the Dissolution, boards displaying the Ten Commandments, the Creed and the Lord's Prayer were nailed over it; indeed, a section known to portray Christ in Glory, with various attendant angels, has been lost since 1829.

Elsewhere, the church is full of interesting details and visitors are well advised to take their time and look at the various features and memorials at their leisure, despite the fact that, as one might expect, Romsey Abbey is very popular with tourists and coach parties, especially from March to September. On no account should the two extremely rare late Saxon roods or crucifixes be missed, with their expressively carved figures and compellingly Saxon appeal. The richly carved Norman capital just before the altar has a particularly graphic battle scene involving angels and decorated with severed limbs and heads reminiscent of the border detail of the Bayeux Tapestry. The grave of Earl Mountbatten is in the south transept, along with a memorial to John St Barbe and his wife which has a playful anagram of their names and a 13th-century marble effigy, with, oddly (perhaps a later repair), a 14th-century canopy.

The manor of **Broadlands** belonged to the abbey before the Dissolution, but was acquired by the St Barbe family, who were active in local and national politics on the Parliamentarian side during the Stuart period and the Civil War. Their Jacobean mansion and grounds were redesigned in 1760 and refashioned by Capability Brown before passing to the Palmerston family, whose third viscount was Prime Minister (1855–8 and 1859–65). It was the home of Lord Louis Mountbatten until his death in 1979 and the estate is now in the hands of his grandson, Lord Romsey.

Normally open to visitors, the house is closed until 2011, but the grounds are still open for special events such as the Romsey Show. Of particular note are the period 18th-century furniture and the collection of English, Dutch and Italian paintings. In the converted stables, there is a dedicated exhibition about Earl Mountbatten and his countess that describes their lives and explains their influential roles in national and international affairs.

To the north-west of Romsey, **Mottisfont**, with its thatched cottages and Georgian houses, admirably comple-ments its picturesque setting by the River Test. It has an old tithe barn and a 12th-century church that contains a Norman chancel, a rare clock mechanism and the finest quantity of 15th-century stained glass in the county. A head of Christ and the flaming sun badge of Edward IV are particularly noteworthy. The village itself offers excellent access for easy walking along well-maintained, wooded estate paths and to the Dun valley.

Mottisfont Abbey is in an idyllic situation by the River Test, amid ancient trees and wonderfully land-scaped gardens. Originally founded as an Augustinian priory in 1201 by William Briwere, one of the Magna Carta barons, it was acquired at the Dissolution by William, Lord Sandys, who converted the premises into a Tudor country house. The north wall of the house can just be identified as the north wall of the original nave, while a beautiful 13th-century undercroft and a section of the chapter house have been skilfully incorporated. Several generations later, in 1706, Sir Richard Mill inherited the estate and converted the building to its present appearance. The eye-catching Drawing Room was created by Rex Whistler in 1938 in the Gothic style and the interior is further enhanced by a collection of 20th-century art, donated by the artist Derek Hill.

Worth a Look

King John's House

In 1927, a private house, comprising old cottages and a Tudor building, previously used as a workhouse in the 18th century, was identified as a hunting lodge built by King John in 1206. However, evidence now suggests that the house, built in about 1230 to 1240, was owned by the Abbess of Romsey and used as a guest-house, probably as 'overflow accommodation'. Built of flint with stone quoins, it has pointed windows and 'dog-tooth' mouldings typical of the 13th century. Its outstanding feature is a series of graffiti, scratched with a dagger, recording the arms and mottoes of about 20 barons who stayed during a royal visit by Edward I in 1306. The small museum displays relics and curios relating to the history of Romsey.

Worth a Brief Look

Statue of Lord Palmerston

(prime minister 1855–8 and 1859–65), who was born at Broadlands – in the Market Place.

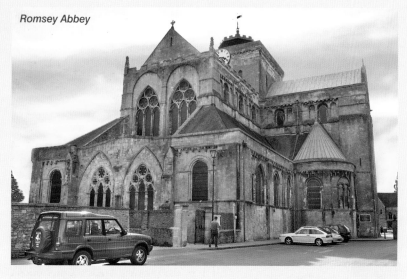

Romsey Abbey

The gardens owe their splendour to the work of Gilbert and Maude Russell, who owned the estate between 1934 and 1957, employing Norah Lindsay and Geoffrey Jellicoe to redesign and completely reconfigure the area around the house. In 1957, the house and gardens were given to the National Trust and in 1972 Graham Stuart Thomas assembled the distinc- tive collection of historic shrub roses in the walled gardens. The grounds offer inspirational vistas and the opportunity for leisurely walks and reflection – but only when the abbey and its grounds are not at peak capacity.

Two miles (3km) north-east of Romsey, **Sir Harold Hillier Gardens**, with its 180 acres (73ha) of careful land- scaping, woodlands and paths, is one of

Romsey - Lord Palmerston

Mottisfont

streams amid the water meadows. The local area has been settled for over 4,000 years and the town is at the intersection of the Roman road from Old Sarum to Winchester and another ancient road running along the Test Valley. It was here that Robert, Earl of Gloucester was captured in 1141 by the forces of King Stephen, covering the retreat from Winchester of his half-sister, the Empress Mathilda.

The town's prosperity grew as a result of its favourable geographical position, especially as a result of cattle and sheep droving. Welsh drovers certainly used the local facilities on their way to sheep fairs and markets in London and the South East. A thatched cottage called 'Drovers House' has the message

Above & Below: Sir Harold Hillier Gardens

the most enjoyable and varied garden experiences in the county, particularly in spring when the azaleas, rhododendrons and magnolias are in full bloom. The gardens contain a collection of over 42,000 plants from temperate regions around the world, based on the work of the founder Sir Harold Hillier from 1953 onwards, as well as 12 National Plant Collections, a Gurkha Memorial Garden and a 650ft (200m) flowering border. Other attractions which make these gardens a first-class family visit include a Bog Garden, a Winter Garden and a Children's Education Garden. There are events and exhibitions all year round, with Art in the Garden (over 200 sculptures) from May to October, and free guided tours on Sundays.

Stockbridge, on the Test midway between Andover to the north and Romsey, means 'the bridge over the river', which divides here into five in Welsh on its wall meaning 'Mature hay, lush pasture, good beer, comfortable beds'. The town was also notorious for its corruption and as a 'rotten borough' before the Great Reform Act of 1832.

This typical market town is notable for its broad main street, which crosses various streams and contains numerous irregular-shaped houses that give the town a quaintly traditional appearance. An old coaching inn, the Grosvenor Hotel with its projecting porch, and the Guildhall, with a clock tower of 1810, stand out.

Just to the north, and next to a particularly pretty village, the celebrated **Longstock Water Garden**s are part of the 3,750-acre (1,500ha) Leckford Estate (owned by the John Lewis Partnership), which includes agricultural land, a fruit farm and woodlands, as well as five miles of the River Test. The main lake of the water gardens was created by accident in 1870, when the owners of Longstock House dredged gravel from the banks of the River Test, to create a private road. In the 1920s, the water was diverted into a central canal and two small lakes and the banks were covered with plants.

Today's gardens cover seven acres (3ha), including two and a half acres (1ha) of lake, which are fed by the Test, to a depth of between three and six feet (1–2m). They are largely the work of John Spedan Lewis, who acquired the property in 1946. In developing the gardens over ten years, the size of the gardens grew to three times their original size. Improvements and the maintenance of the unusual habitat have been in progress ever since and the intricate patterns and cleverly arranged

> ## Worth a Look
>
> Old St Peter's Church is at the east end of town and, with only the chancel remaining, is the mortuary chapel for the graveyard. It is of Norman origin, but many of its fittings have been transferred to new St Peter's in the centre of the town. However, if you are passing the old church, it is worth a look, together with the lyrical epitaph to one John Buckett, the landlord of the King's Head Inn until 1802.

water and horticultural features reveal a host of pleasant surprises and associations. Most of the hard work is done by hand by wader-clad gardeners, who use floating zinc baths as wheelbarrows, and there is a thriving nursery from which plants can be bought. The International Water Lily Society has voted Longstock 'the finest water garden in the world'.

Another fine garden may be found just to the south of Stockbridge. Built on a hill overlooking the River Test, **Houghton Lodge** was probably a fishing lodge dating from the late 18th century, an example of a cottage orné or rural retreat. Both the Lodge and its gardens are in an idyllic setting and the horticultural arrangements are delightful and imaginative. Among the numerous informal and formal settings, there are greenhouses, a kitchen garden and a modern hydroponicum, where plants are grown without soil, as well as opportunities to walk through the extensive, adjacent meadows.

Paulton's Family Theme Park, on the edge of the New Forest and on the banks of the Cadnam River, is probably the all-round best day out for families with children in the whole of the county. Very popular with local people as well as visitors, it offers a bewildering array of over 50 attractions and rides on one site, with most attractions included in the entry price. There are thrills and spills rides (such as Cobra, Stinger and Wave Runner), as well as the more gentle variety (such as the Tea Cup and Flying Saucer rides), together with plenty of opportunities to let off steam on various attractions. As well as exotic birds and animals, including meerkats and penguins, there is a Land of Dinosaurs section and a Village Life Museum, backed up by a multitude of refreshment outlets and participation activities. The latest additions include The Edge, a decidedly quick, spinning roller-coaster ride, and Wave Kingdom, an 8,500 sq ft (800 sq m) play pool with jets and sprays (motto: 'over 20 ways to get wet'). Take your towels and swimming gear!

To the East

Botley has been a settlement at least since the tenth century and was a small port on the line of an old Roman road, which crossed a ford over the River Hamble. Inns later provided hospitality and refuge for travellers when the tide was high and the village specialised in parchment making and milling. Today, it has a handsome main street fronted by several attractive houses of various dates and the remains of what would have been coaching inns, of which only two, the Bugle and the Dolphin, survive. It has a striking market-hall, built in 1849, which has a portico supported by four large Portland stone piers.

Between 1806 and 1820, Botley was the home of the journalist, farmer and radical politician William Cobbett, of 'Rural Rides' fame, who described Botley as 'the most delightful village in the world'. A house and cottage in Church Lane are all that remain of his holding, but there is a memorial stone to him in the Square.

The Cistercian house of **Netley Abbey**, on the east bank of Southampton Water, was founded in 1239 by Henry III and was occupied by monks from the older house at Beaulieu. It was frequently in financial difficulties because of the responsibilities of its position (maintaining a navigation light and rescue facilities) on the coast, the threat of French raiding and the constant demands made on its hospitality by mariners. At its dissolution in 1536, it was actually given a good report by the commissioners and reported as 'giving great relief and comfort to the King's subjects and travelling strangers'. Even so, the abbey was dissolved and acquired by Sir William Paulet, the Marquis of Winchester. Parts of the abbey church and conventual buildings were incorporated into a residence, whose red-brick foundations are visible among the ruins. In the 18th century, the site was sold to a Southampton developer named Taylor who proceeded to dismantle the buildings, but was killed by falling masonry. The demolition promptly ceased and the project was abandoned, although around 1,700 more stones were removed for building works, including those at St Mary's Church, Southampton.

Despite the depredations of time

The Jumping Bean at Paultons Park

a fashionable mock ruin in Cranbury Park, near Otterbourne. On the south side are the remains of the cloister, which is 115ft (35m) square, and among other offices and buildings normally associated with a typical Cistercian abbey, there are the ruins of a chapter house, the monks' dormitory, the lay-brothers' quarters and, slightly apart, the abbot's lodging house. This is a two-storey building with a vaulted hall and an attached chapel.

Nearby is **Netley Castle**, one of Henry VIII's coastal forts, built between 1542 and 1545 under the direction of Sir William Paulet, the owner of the abbey at the time. Manned until 1647, it was converted into a private house in 1881. In 1938 it was acquired as a convalescent home, but was sold again in the 1990s and remains in private hands.

and quarrying for stone, a good deal survives of the mainly 13th-century Early English style abbey, particularly the church, whose 215ft (65m) nave, chancel, aisles and south transept remain. The south transept, with chapels that have retained their vaulting, still stands, but the north transept has disappeared, removed in the 18th century to form

The land now occupied by the **Royal Victoria Country Park** was the site and grounds of the **Royal Victoria Military Hospital**, a vast building with a frontage over a third of a mile (half a kilometre) long, which was built

Longstock

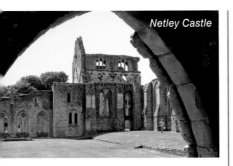
Netley Castle

between 1856 and 1863. Its construction was ordered on the insistence of Queen Victoria after the Crimean War and the Queen herself laid the foundation stone, under which was placed an original Victoria Cross. The hospital has since been demolished, but the medal was recovered. Florence Nightingale, on her return from the Crimea, was deeply critical of its design – '*the comfort and recovery of the patients have been sacrificed to the vanity of the architect*.' The grandiose building was visually attractive, but was not constructed with the needs of the patients in mind. Corridors had been built on the sea-facing front of the building, leaving the wards facing the inner courtyard with little light and air. Ventilation and sanitation were poor, with unpleasant odours circulating around the vast building. Nevertheless, improvements were made over time and the hospital was in constant use throughout the period covering the Boer Wars, the Great War and World War II, until it fell into disuse around 1958, owing to the prohibitive cost of maintenance in peacetime. A large fire occurred in 1963 and the building was demolished in 1966. The separate former asylum was taken over by Hampshire Constabulary as a training headquarters and the officers' mess has been converted into private apartments.

Worth a Look

The Royal Victoria Country Park itself comprises 200 acres (80ha) of mature woodland and grassy parkland, as well as a small shingle and shell beach. The whole park is criss-crossed with trails and paths that allow access to woodlands and marshy areas supporting a variety of wildlife and plants. Other amenities include a tea room (sited in a former YMCA) and a miniature narrow-gauge railway (the Royal Victoria Railway) on the site. There is plenty of car parking space and a footpath to and from Netley Station.

In addition, the hospital chapel has survived and today acts as an informative visitor and heritage centre, where the history of the hospital is exhibited and memorable views of Southampton Water can be experienced from the top of its 150ft (45m) tower.

In *A Study in Scarlet*, the first Sherlock Holmes book, Dr Watson claims that he had been trained at Netley.

Royal Victoria Country Park

Places to Visit

Broadlands

www.broadlands.net
The house is currently undergoing a major renovation programme and will be closed for several years.

Romsey Abbey

SO51 8EN
☎ 01794 513125
www.romseyabbey.org
Open daily from 8am–6pm. Donations welcome.

King John's House

Church Street, Romsey, SO51 8BT
☎ 01794 512200
www.kingjohnshouse.org.uk
Open Mon–Sat all year.

Mottisfont Abbey

Mottisfont, Near Romsey, SO51 0LP
☎ 01794 340757
www.nationaltrust.org.uk
Open daily Mar to Oct. Closed some Fri.

Netley Abbey

SO31 5FB
☎ 02392 378291
www.english-heritage.org.uk
Open daily Apr to Sept 10am–6pm; Weekends only Oct to Mar 10am–3pm, closed 24–26 Dec & 1 Jan. Admission free.

Paultons Park

Ower, Near Romsey, SO51 6AL
☎ 023 8081 4442
www.paultonspark.co.uk
Open daily 10am–5pm from Apr to Sept, restricted opening Feb & Mar, Oct to Dec. Closed Jan. Special Christmas event: Santa's Christmas Wonderland must be pre-booked.

Art Gallery

Civic Centre, Commercial Road, SO14 7LP
☎ 023 8083 2277
www.southampton.gov.uk/art
Mon–Fri: 10am–6pm; Sat–Sun: 11am–6pm; Admission free.

God's House Tower Museum of Archaeology

Tower House, Winkle St, Southampton, SO14 2NY
☎ 023 8063 5904
www.southampton.gov.uk
Open all year Tue–Sat from 10am–4pm & Sun from1–4pm. Closed Christmas & New Year.

Hall of Aviation (Solent Sky)

Albert Road, South Southampton, SO14 3FR
☎ 023 8063 5830
www.spitfireonline.co.uk
Open daily all year except Mon from 10am–5pm. Closed 24–26 Dec, 31 Dec & 1 Jan.

Maritime Museum

The Wool House, Town Quay, Southampton, SO14 2AR
☎ 023 8022 3941
www.southampton.gov.uk
Open all year Tue–Sat from 10am–4pm & Sun from 1–4pm. Closed Christmas and New Year.

Medieval Merchant's House

58 French St, Southampton, SO14 0AT
www.english-heritage.org.uk
Open Apr to Sept on Sun from 12pm–5pm.

Tudor House Museum & Garden

Bugle Street, Southampton, SO14 2AD
The museum is currently undergoing a major renovation programme and will be closed for several years. For latest details check the website:
www.southampton.gov.uk/leisure/localhistoryandheritage/museums-galleries/tudorhouse

Titchfield Abbey

Titchfield, PO15 5RA
www.english-heritage.org.uk
Open daily from 10am–5pm (4pm in winter). Closed 24–26 Dec and 1 Jan. Admission free.

GARDENS

Mottisfont Abbey Gardens

Mottisfont, SO51 0LP
☎ 01794 340757
www.nationaltrust.org.uk
Open daily Mar to Oct. Closed some Fri. Open daily 11am–8pm in Jun for Rose Garden.

Houghton Lodge Gardens & Hydroponicum

Near Stockbridge, SO20 6LQ
☎ 01264 810502
www.houghtonlodge.co.uk
Open Mar to Oct every day except Wed from 10am–5pm.

Longstock Park Water Garden

Near Stockbridge, SO20 6JF
☎ 01264 810904
www.longstockpark.co.uk
Open for charity on the 1st and 3rd Sun of the month Apr to Sept 2pm–5pm.

Sir Harold Hiller Garden

Jermyns Lane, Ampfield, Romsey, Hampshire, SO51 0QA
☎ 01794 369318
www.hilliergardens.org.uk
Open daily except Christmas Day and Boxing Day from 10am–5pm (6pm in summer).

The National Gardens Scheme

Visitors enjoy access to private gardens which are not normally open to the public and the money raised supports a range of national and local charities. Opening dates and times of the gardens are available on the website: www.ngs.org.uk.

COUNTRY PARKS

Itchen Valley Country Park

Allington Lane, West End, Near Eastleigh, SO30 3HQ
☎ 023 8046 6091
www.eastleigh.gov.uk
Open daily all year round from 8.30am until dusk. Admission free. Car parking charge.

Royal Victoria Country Park

Netley Abbey, SO31 5GA
☎ 023 8045 5157
www.hants.gov.uk/rvcp
Park opens daily. Heritage and Information Centre open from 10am. Small admission charge.

4. Portsmouth & the East

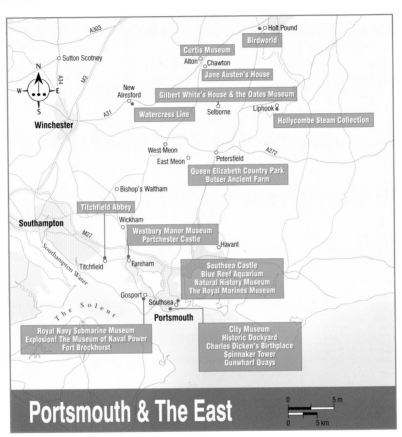

Portsmouth & The East

This area comprises the historic naval city of Portsmouth, a seemingly unending ribbon of residential and commercial development along the Solent shore towards Southampton and ready access to a landscape of undulating chalk farmland and breathtaking downs, as well as prosperous towns and tidy villages to the north and east. Within comfortable commuting distance of London, it has excellent communications in all directions and, especially during the holiday periods, is a lively, sometimes brash and boisterous corner of the county.

However, especially to the east of the busy A3 London road and in the river valleys of the Meon and the Hamble, the familiar charm of rural Hampshire prevails. Similarly, the area around Petersfield, taking in Selborne and the Sussex border, represents some of the most diverse unspoilt countryside in the county, with excellent opportunities for walking, recreation and getting away from it all.

Very few people are aware that **Portsmouth** is built on an island and that, with a population of about 240,000, it is one of the most densely populated cities in the United Kingdom. With a familiar reputation as the country's pre-eminent naval port and its long historic and cultural association with the Royal Navy, the city has a great deal to offer visitors, not only because of its historical and nautical interests, but also in relation to its leisure and entertainment facilities. The city is backed by immediate access to open countryside and its ferries offer numerous easy routes and opportunities (from the one-day trip to the extended stay) to enjoy the extensive and undoubted attractions of the Isle of Wight. Its location alone, fronting onto the Solent and the Isle of Wight, is worth a significant detour, especially when viewed from the crest of Portsdown Hill, to the north of the city, or from the extensive esplanade that stretches along Southsea seafront for more than three miles (5km). The City Council has linked many of its historic attractions together with a Millennium Walkway, which runs from the Historic Dockyard along the seafront into Old Portsmouth and along the existing fortifications to Clarence Pier. It is marked by distinctive lamp posts and a chain motif set into the ground. At the time of writing, Portsmouth Harbour was being proposed for Word Heritage Site status.

Most of Portsmouth's attractions are grouped in four main areas. **Old Portsmouth** and its High Street, clustered around the entrance to the harbour, contain much of the old fortified town of Portsmouth. The **Historic Dockyard**, within the naval base complex, is home to three historic ships and a range of maritime heritage attractions, as well as proximity to a major retail outlet centre. **Southsea seafront** and common combine outstanding sea views of the Solent along a 3-mile (5km) esplanade that gives access to a variety of leisure, cultural and recreational opportunities. Finally, the **main shopping centre** is located in Commercial Road close to Portsmouth and Southsea station, although there are retail alternatives at Gunwharf Quays and Southsea.

In Roman times, the low-lying island (Portsea) on which Portsmouth is built comprised extensive marshland, which seems to have been considered unsuitable for permanent habitation and occupation. As a result, when a fort was needed in the late third century by the Romans, a site at the top of the harbour was chosen on a promontory that had previously been occupied by a prehistoric settlement, which later became Portchester.

At the time of Domesday in 1086, Portsea Island contained three small agricultural villages – Buckland, Copnor and Fratton. Its rise to prominence as Portsmouth started at the end of the 12th century with a merchant named Jean de Gisors. After purchasing the manor of Buckland, he began to develop his land on the south-western part of Portsea Island at the entrance to the harbour. Portsmouth grew up as a small trading and fishing port clustered around a small spit of land near the entrance to the harbour. At some stage between 1180 and 1186, he gave Southwick Priory a site on which to build a chapel 'in honour of the glorious martyr Thomas of Canterbury, formerly Archbishop'. By 1194, the settlement was important and rich enough to be granted a charter by Richard I. The first docks are thought to have been constructed by the royal surveyor William of Wrotham in 1212, but, for most of the Middle Ages, Portsmouth played a distinctly second fiddle to Southampton as a trading port.

Its position as the country's foremost naval port began with the building of a primitive dry dock in 1495, under Henry VII – it is recorded that the first ship to use the dock was the *Sovereign* a year later – and the subsequent expansion of the navy under Henry VIII. Further growth of shipbuilding and ship repair was rapid under Henry VIII and Elizabeth I and by the time of the Civil War in the 17th century Portsmouth was considered to be one of the most important military and naval bases in the country. During the subsequent wars against the Dutch, the French and the Spanish, the area of the Dockyard and the range of its facilities grew still further to provide the ships and the massive support required to fight wars on a global scale during the Napoleonic Wars and beyond. The Dockyard and the city were in the forefront of the naval and military effort in two world wars and the Falklands conflict of 1982.

Portsmouth remains to this day the country's premier naval base, with warships undergoing maintenance in the dockyard and routinely visible at sea in Spithead and the Solent. Aircraft carriers, destroyers, frigates and minehunters are based here and several entries and departures take place daily, mostly in the early morning and late afternoon. The News, Portsmouth's local newspaper, and its associated website (www.portsmouth.co.uk) have up-to-date details of naval movements and the best vantage point is the Round Tower in Old Portsmouth. There are also regular ferry movements, both to the Isle of Wight and to France and Spain.

Old Portsmouth & the High Street

The High Street formed the main thoroughfare of the fortified city and today lies at the centre of what is known as Old Portsmouth. The area was heavily bombed in World War II and very few historic buildings have survived.

The entry to the High Street is dominated by the former Cambridge Barracks, which now houses the independent Portsmouth Grammar School, while a little further along is Buckingham House, where in 1628, when it was called the 'Spotted Dog', George Villiers, Duke of Buckingham was murdered.

Portsmouth is unusual among British

Worth a Visit

Before proceeding to the High Street, the Portsmouth City Museum, a short distance along Museum Road is worth a visit. Housed in a former barracks building, it houses a representative collection of objects and pictures that present the story of Portsmouth from the earliest times up to the present. The building also houses the City's archives and the unique Lancelyn Green collection of Sherlock Holmes memorabilia.

Worth a Look

A short distance in the other direction, towards the Dockyard, is the Landport Gate, which was the main entrance to Portsmouth from London at the north-east limit of the old town. This gate was erected in 1760 and remains on its original site.

---

cities in having two cathedrals: the Anglican cathedral of St Thomas and the **Roman Catholic Cathedral** of St John the Evangelist.

Portsmouth's Anglican **Cathedral** was built as a chapel for Southwick Priory around 1185 and grew to be a parish church during the medieval period, despite being raided in 1338 and closed during Portsmouth's 60-year excommunication in the 15th century. Heavily damaged by gunfire from Parliamentary Gosport during the Civil War, it was rebuilt between 1691 and 1702. when the main tower and its cupola were added. At the same time, the church bells were recast from those that used to hang in the Roman lighthouse at Dover. When it became a cathedral in 1927, the nave was extensively remodelled, with enlargement work beginning on the west front in 1930. This construction was suspended at the start of the Second World War and was not completed until 1991.

The cathedral today is an intriguing hotchpotch of architectural features and contents, as well as, appropriately, a large number of naval and maritime associations and memorials. The earliest parts remaining today are the two transepts and the former medieval choir which now forms the sanctuary behind the altar. The former nave is now the choir and the nave extends to the west as a result of the 17th-century modifications and the enlargement work of the late 1980s.

At the end of the High Street is the **Square Tower** built on the orders of Henry VII in 1494, with a bust of the future Charles I, commemorating his safe return from an escapade to Spain in 1623 when he tried to gain a sneak preview of a Spanish princess whom his father, James I, wanted him to marry. Originally serving as the fortified residence of the Governor of Portsmouth, it was also designed to house guns on its roof. It was subsequently a gunpowder magazine and, in 1779, was converted for use as a meat store. It still retains its original Tudor features.

It is probably a good idea at this stage to proceed along Broad Street, which bears to the right onto Portsmouth Point, and walk to the end of the road. This part of the city, outside the fortified area, used to be notorious for its brothels, drinking houses and bad behaviour in the days of fighting sail. It is a convenient and pleasant spot today, both to enjoy a couple of good pubs (with food), the Still and West and the Spice Island Inn, and to admire the view up harbour. Between 1840 and 1959, a floating bridge used to operate to Gosport from this point. Another option is to turn aside into the small inlet of the Camber, the original port of Portsmouth, but now full of small boats and fishing vessels, and visit the Bridge Tavern.

Shortly after a devastating raid on Southampton and Portsmouth by the French and Genoese in 1338, the area around the Camber and the harbour entrance was quickly fortified with earthworks and moats. Turning back along Broad Street, one comes to the **Round Tower**, built in masonry as a replacement for a wooden predecessor in 1426 and rebuilt in the reign of Queen Elizabeth I. Although the Tower is not open to the public, steps lead to a first-class viewpoint at the top, from where all movements in and out of the harbour can be observed at particularly close quarters. Next to the tower is the site of the capstan that was used to raise and lower the great chain that spanned the harbour entrance from the time of Henry VIII.

The visitor can now take an enjoyable stroll back towards the Square Tower along the seafront and see the fortifications. From the Round Tower, a Millennium Walk takes the pedestrian through 18 Gun Battery (1680) to the Square Tower (passing memorials to the First Fleet to Australia in 1780 and the Falklands War of 1982) and then to 10 Gun Battery (1670) and the Saluting Platform (1568), a broad terrace above Grand Parade, where there is a statue in memory of Lord Nelson. The Millennium Walk continues to the Spur Redoubt (1680), a moat (1680) and the Long Curtain, a grass embankment (1730), which show what the whole circuit of Portsmouth's formidable artillery fortifications would have looked like.

The **Spur Redoubt** contains a tunnel which passes through Long Curtain, which is thought to have been the route taken by Nelson before he embarked for the campaign that led to the Battle of Trafalgar. At the landward

Portsmouth's Fortifications

By the start of the 18th century, Portsmouth was enclosed in a complex, constantly updated range of earth, stone and brick fortifications and moats that recall the surviving defences of Berwick-upon-Tweed, with their star-shaped, angled bastions and ravelins. Through the course of the 19th century, improvements in the range, trajectory and accuracy of ordnance, especially the introduction of rifled guns and armoured warships, made the defences of Old Portsmouth redundant. A tight ring of modern forts along the crest of Portsdown Hill, at sea in the Solent and on the Gosport peninsula was built from the 1860s onwards, but almost all Portsmouth's defensive structures were demolished in 1876.

The four forts that can be seen in the Solent were built in the 1860s to defend Portsmouth and the Solent against possible attack. In the Crimean war, the Royal Navy had been surprised by the effectiveness of the Russian forts at Sebastopol and later by the production of the world's first ironclad, the French *La Gloire*, in 1859 and the introduction of rifled guns that offered greater range. The Royal Navy responded by building the ironclads *Warrior, Black Prince, Defence* and *Resistance* while plans for fortifications at key ports and points along the south and east coasts of England were drafted. As Britain's pre-eminent naval port, it was considered that Portsmouth needed an all-round defence, not only against an enemy attacking from seaward, but also against one that had landed elsewhere and was attacking the city from the land. A comprehensive system of forts and artillery batteries was built in the 1860s around Gosport, Portsmouth and the Isle of Wight to strengthen existing arrangements at a cost of roughly £1.5 million.

The four Solent sea forts were built to cover the deep-water passage through Spithead. The two largest are *No Man's Land* and *Horse Sand*, with the smaller *Spitbank* and *St Helen's*, and all were constructed between 1868 and 1871 with a complex layered structure of armour and heavy masonry on granite foundations. *St Helen's* eventually mounted two 10-inch, 18-ton guns and four 12.5-inch, 38-ton guns on its seaward side.

Other forts in the system, built at the same time, can be seen at one-mile intervals along the crest of Portsdown Hill above Portsmouth. On the Isle of Wight, the observant visitor will see other traces of the system, particularly guarding the Needles Channel (*Fort Victoria, Fort Albert, Golden Hill* and a host of minor batteries on the Freshwater Peninsula). Other elements may be seen at Sandown, Bembridge, Yaverland and Puckpool, protecting the eastern approaches to the Isle of Wight.

end of the tunnel, a path leads to a cottage, which was originally the guard house of King William's Gate (1833) which stood on this site.

The **Domus Dei** (Hospital of Saint Nicholas) was an almshouse and hospice run by a Master, six nuns and six monks, which was established in 1212 by Peter des Roches, the Bishop of Winchester. In 1450, it was the scene of the murder by mutinous and unpaid seamen of Adam Moleyns, the Bishop of Chichester and an unpopular advisor to Henry VI. In 1540, like other religious buildings, the hospice was acquired by King Henry VIII and used as an armoury and gunpowder store until 1560 when it became the home of the local military governor. Its chapel – the church that survives – stayed in use and in 1662 it saw the wedding by proxy of King Charles II and Catherine of Braganza. At the end of the 17th century, it fell into disrepair, but was restored in 1867 as the Royal Garrison Church for the Army personnel stationed in the city. In January 1941, the church was partially destroyed by German bombs and lost its roof, although the chancel survives. Its graveyard holds the tomb of General Sir Charles Napier, famous as the conqueror of Sind province in India and author of the punning single-word dispatch 'peccavi' (meaning 'I have sinned' in Latin) announcing his achievement.

The Historic Dockyard

The Historic Dockyard is accessed from the Main Dockyard gate on the Hard, in full view of *HMS Warrior* and adjacent to the coach and bus station and Portsmouth Harbour Railway Station. The short passenger ferry to and from Gosport and the Fast Cat service to the Isle of Wight also operate from this point.

Much of the pleasure of a visit to the Historic Dockyard is derived from being able to see not only historic ships, but also their modern counterparts, from aircraft carriers to mine-hunters, alongside and under way nearby. Although it is not possible to visit modern warships and auxiliaries except during special 'Meet the Navy' events (usually during the summer), a scheduled boat trip around the harbour – Warships by Water – allows visitors to gain a close-up view of the ships in port. In addition, there are daily movements by naval vessels in and out of harbour.

The area of the Dockyard open to the public comprises a series of mainly brick buildings from the period of the Seven Years' War (1756–63) onwards. Most of the existing premises date from later in the 18th century, notably the extensive stores depots (1778) which are on the route to *HMS Victory* and the Great Ropehouse (rebuilt in 1776 after an arson attack and just outside the public area), which at 1,095 feet (334m) is one of the longest continuous buildings in the world. Within the site, there is a range of themed shops, selling a wide variety of naval, maritime and historic merchandise, and several refreshment outlets.

HMS Victory

HMS Victory was built using 3,000 oak trees at Chatham dockyard between 1759 and 1765 and first saw action off Ushant in 1778. Although she could

Victory Gallery

hold up to 850 men, at Trafalgar her ship's company was 820. She led the attack on the combined French and Spanish Fleet at the Battle of Trafalgar, where, in the thick of the fighting, she lost much of her rigging and sustained serious hull damage. Consequently, she had to be towed to Gibraltar before return to Britain and further war service. Her last commission was as flagship to Admiral Sir James de Saumarez in the Baltic and she was paid off from active service at Portsmouth in 1812. She was held in reserve from 1816 to 1824 and remained afloat and at anchor in the harbour in various roles until 1922. On 12 January 1922, she was taken into dry dock so that she could be restored to her 1805 configuration and in 1928 she was first opened to the public. She remains in commission today and is the flagship of the Second Sea Lord.

This immaculately presented and

Dressing up on the Mary Rose

carefully preserved fighting ship is probably the most rewarding and fascinating visitor attraction in Hampshire. Although much of her original structure and rigging has been progressively replaced over the years, it is impossible not to be moved and impressed by the sight and experience of the oldest commissioned warship in the world. Dedicated scholarship and painstaking attention to detail over many years have ensured that all aspects of the ship are as authentic as

HMS Victory

possible and she is laid out as she would have been equipped and configured in action in 1805. Visitors are able to take a genuinely enthralling guided tour around the upper deck, the gun decks (both fully equipped with cannons, weapons and equipment of the time), Nelson's Great Cabin and many of the between decks areas, such as the hold, the powder magazine and the cockpit where Nelson died. The galley and sick bay have also been restored and put on display.

Visitors will be admitted either on a guided tour or on a free-flow system. The guided tour system is in operation throughout quieter periods of the year, with times allocated on entry to the Historic Dockyard Visitors' Centre on a first-come, first-served basis.

HMS Warrior was the first iron-hulled, armour-plated warship in the world, powered by both sails and steam technology, after it was discovered that the French had developed an ironclad warship, La Gloire. When completed in

October 1861, *Warrior* was the largest, fastest, most armoured and most armoured warship in the world, combining for the first time in one hull steam engines, rifled breech-loading guns, iron construction, iron armour and propeller drive, all designed to outclass, outrun and outgun any other warship. Unfortunately, her revolutionary design provoked an arms race and, although never used in battle, she was obsolete within ten years. Between 1929 and 1979 she was an oil storage hulk at Pembroke Dock in West Wales, before being purchased by the Maritime Trust and restored to her former glory at Hartlepool, arriving at her present berth in Portsmouth in 1987. Visitors can now walk around the ship whose remarkable restoration, internal fittings and equipment show how she would have been in the 1860s, with a wealth of original and replica items on show.

The **Mary Rose** was built in 1509, rebuilt in 1536 and was one of the major capital ships of Henry VIII's navy. She was leading part of the English fleet that was defending Portsmouth from attack by a French fleet in July 1545. Owing to a series of mishaps and errors while she was hurriedly manoeuvring to engage the enemy, she capsized rapidly, just outside Portsmouth harbour, with the loss of almost all her crew and soldiers, in full view of the king, who was ashore at Southsea Castle.

Despite the rediscovery of the ship in 1836, the technology was not available to recover anything from the site until the location of the hull in 1971. In 1982, after careful evaluation of the site and the removal of many artefects, the hull was finally lifted in a remarkable operation and placed in preservation next to *HMS Victory*. A special museum was created to exhibit the huge range of finds, which include cannons, longbows and a wide variety of personal and sea-going items. It is the only surviving preserved warship from the 16th century.

Because of its long immersion in seawater, the half section of the hull has to be sprayed continuously with preservative and can only be viewed from behind glass screens. Visitors who forget the age of the ship and its miraculous preservation in the conditions prevailing in the Solent might feel that the Mary Rose is not as impressive as the other two historic ships on view. However, the ship needs to be viewed in conjunction with the outstanding exhibition and range of original artefacts recovered from the wreck site in the museum and in the light of the context that the preserved hull provides. The museum has a thriving and influential research section that is constantly producing fresh insights about the ship, her people and her last battle.

The Royal Naval Museum

Despite its name and perhaps reflecting its original purpose and bequests, this museum is overwhelmingly devoted to life at sea in the Royal Navy of Nelson's day, a task which it achieves remarkably well. This is the absolutely must-see museum for all those who have a fascination for the way of life portrayed in the novels of C.S. Forester, Patrick O'Brian or Douglas Reeman, or who wish to know a little more about an inspiring period of British history.

It comprises several different, but connected galleries.

• **The Victory Gallery** provides a detailed insight into the life of the ship and the men who served in her, as well as models, paintings and period exhibits relating to the Battle of Trafalgar and Nelson. Basic hands-on exhibits, audio-visual presentations and interactive displays show how the ship was sailed and fought, while a short walk-through display, with realistic sights and sounds, explains the events before and during the Battle of Trafalgar, culminating in the spectacular panorama of the battle painted by the marine artist W.L.Wyllie. Other attractions include a large number of ship's figureheads, Nelson's funeral barge, model ships and an outdoor public platform with a good view of the harbour and its shipping.

• **The Lambert McCarthy Gallery** contains personal effects and furniture from Nelson's life on board *Victory* and his home with Emma Hamilton at Merton.

• **The Douglas Morris Gallery** tells the story of the Napoleonic wars and the last days of sail, together with the often forgotten period of exploration and expansion of Empire that followed.

• **The Wyllie Gallery** deals with aspects of the Victorian Navy while the **Lewin Gallery** gives an insight into World Wars I and II.

• **The Sailing Navy Gallery** is in one of the 18th-century storehouses which has floors made from the timbers of captured French and Spanish ships. The gallery is designed to stimulate both adults and children by presenting, in an interactive and hands-on way, a balanced view of the sailing Navy and by dispelling some of the myths about life onboard. An interactive computer allows visitors to feel how it was to sail a 74-gun warship and there is a chance to handle weapons of the time.

• '**Sea Your History: 20th Century Royal Navy**' demonstrates how the Royal Navy has been operating over the past 100 years, with material from the Royal Naval Museum itself and exhibits borrowed from the Fleet Air Arm Museum, the Royal Marines Museum, and the Royal Navy Submarine Museum. A Modern Navy display describes the ships, operations and technologies of today's fleet.

Nearby, **Gunwharf Quays** combines waterfront and high-rise residential development (note the building appropriately known locally as the 'Lipstick') and a vibrant leisure, commercial and entertainment complex. As a retail outlet centre, it is a very popular destination throughout the year and can be very crowded in the holiday periods. Built on the site of *HMS Vernon*, the former Royal Navy anti-submarine and mine warfare establishment, the site is home to many high street retailers among the 100 or so outlets, together with a 14-screen cinema complex, a casino and a tenpin Bowlplex Centre. Nightclubs cater for a range of tastes and requirements and over 30 cafés, bars and restaurants offer a considerable water's edge choice of refreshment and recreation. An Express by Holiday Inn hotel is also on site.

Within Gunwharf Quays, at 558ft (170m), the **Spinnaker Tower** is two and a half times the height of Nelson's Column and has the largest glass floor in Europe. It was planned as the centrepiece of the regeneration of Portsmouth

Harbour and was originally scheduled for opening in 1999, ahead of the Millennium. It was finally completed in October 2005, after a succession of delays, cost overruns and technical failures and once Portsmouth City Council had contributed £11.1 million to ensure its completion. However, since its opening, the Spinnaker Tower has proved extremely popular and its triple observation deck allows a 320° view over the local area and a nominal

Portsmouth Historic Dockyard

Worth a Look

The Trafalgar Sail Exhibition – this shows the only surviving sail from *HMS Victory* at the Battle of Trafalgar, complete with shot holes and action damage. There is an audio and lighting presentation, together with the story of the sail from its manufacture.

The Dockyard Apprentices' Museum – an understated, but fascinating exhibition of techniques, skills and tools required to service and sustain a fighting navy in the past, right up to recent times.

Action Stations – a host of multimedia experiences, technological demonstrations and interactive games that allow both adults and children to pit their wits against some of the problems faced by modern commanders at sea, as well as simulator rides and science quests.

Worth a Look (When You Can)

The Block Mills

Not far from *Victory* and occasionally open for guided tours are buildings specially constructed to accommodate the revolutionary machinery devised by Marc Brunel, the father of Isambard, for the manufacture of wooden blocks for the Royal Navy. At the start of the 19th century, the Royal Navy needed a huge number of blocks – a typical line of battle ship needed about 1,000 different blocks to work the rigging. These buildings were adapted and equipped between 1802 and 1805 to hold three series of block-making machines, each designed to make a range of block sizes. As a result, by 1808, 130,000 blocks a year were produced. A project is under way to ensure the buildings and remaining machinery are preserved and restored.

---

horizon of 23 miles (37km), taking in the Solent and its harbours, the Isle of Wight and the South Downs.

Southsea

Southsea developed rapidly in the 19th century once technology had been found to drain the marshy ground to the east of the town, most of which consisted of disused marshland and tidal inlets with areas of poor grazing land. At first, from 1809, houses were built to the east of the fortified town primarily for employees of the Dockyard and for retired naval and military officers before more general development catered for people of all occupations. The most fashionable parts were built to the south-east, close to the modern shopping district at Palmerston Road, and much of the building was the direct result of aggressive speculation from 1835 to 1860 by Thomas Owen, an architect, builder and businessman of great acumen and ambition. Although much has been lost to German bombing, there are many remaining

examples of terraces and houses that reveal his imaginative and original designs.

From 1865, with the coming of the railway, almost all Southsea's large hotels were built to accommodate increasing numbers of middle-class tourists and the area was expanding rapidly to house the dependants and relations of the many military and naval personnel stationed in and around Portsmouth. By the 1880s, the Great Morass was being drained, the railway had been extended to the seafront at Southsea and the suburban area had expanded virtually to its present limits.

A wide, accessible promenade extends all the way along the southern part of Portsea Island from Old Portsmouth via Southsea Castle to Eastney and the entrance to Langstone Harbour. With a host of divertingly interesting features to take in en route and spectacular sea views across the Solent, this is, despite its proximity to road traffic on one side and summer crowds on the beach, one of the outstanding walks in

Hampshire. Cultural attractions, open spaces and tacky commercialism mix almost seamlessly, but the route can be accessed at any point and refreshments of all kinds are available at regular intervals. Its most remarkable feature is its Common, which has resisted development, because it was owned by the Crown between 1785 and 1923 and was required for military exercises and training – and, in the earlier years, to enable a clear line of fire at enemy ships.

Southsea Castle was one of a chain of fortifications constructed by Henry VIII around the coast of England to protect the country from possible attack by France and Spain after his break with the pope. Similar fortifications can be found in Hampshire at Calshot and Hurst castles, as well as at Yarmouth on the Isle of Wight, all designed to withstand cannon fire and sited to protect, with their own guns, vital approaches to the Solent and Southampton Water; Southsea was, and still is, positioned to cover the only deep-water channel into and out of Portsmouth and was built in a hurry in 1544 because Henry VIII feared an imminent French attack. Just after its completion in 1545, the king was at the castle when he witnessed at close hand the accidental loss of the *Mary Rose* during a sea battle against the French.

At the time of the Civil War in 1642, the castle was captured by Parliamentary troops, for the first and only time in its history. In 1665, Charles II subsequently ordered a leading international military engineer, Bernard de Gomme, to put in hand major improvements to the city's fortifications and to the castle's design and capability, but in 1759 the castle was damaged by an accidental explosion. Between 1813 and 1814, reconstruction was again undertaken during the Napoleonic Wars, including the counterscarp gallery and tunnel across the moat, although between 1844 and 1850, the castle was being used as a military prison. In the 1820s, a lighthouse was built, which is still in service today, and at the time of the construction of the chain of 'Palmerston folly' forts in the 1860s, the east and west batteries were completed, with vastly improved 6-inch and 9.2-inch guns replacing the original armaments in 1899.

A visit to Southsea Castle includes an interesting 'Story of Portsmouth' exhibition, a chance to view the Fort Cumberland Guard Museum (an 18th-century re-enactment society) and an exhibition that explains the history of the castle. From the top of the keep, there are sweeping views of the Solent and Portsmouth. Castle Field, in front of the castle, is often used for fairs, music concerts and events. On the other side of the Common opposite the castle is the main shopping centre of Southsea, with a full range of high street shops and two department stores.

Clarence Pier was built in 1860, in order to accommodate steamship traffic operating in the Solent and across to the Isle of Wight. It later had a striking Victorian octagonal pavilion, a café, sundeck, shops and a concourse hall, which made it a major attraction. Unfortunately, during the Second World War, it was hit by German bombs and totally destroyed. Today, one can hardly see that this pier used to extend out into the sea as the present structure (completed in 1961) runs along the beach and is – uniquely – wider than it is long. It is now covered by a gaggle of gaudy attractions that together are probably the largest amusement park on the south coast, with the usual rides, 'kiss-me-quick' aspects and slot-machine activities.

Opposite the esplanade on the common between the funfair and the **Blue Reef Aquarium** is the **Naval Memorial**, which remembers those officers and ratings from Portsmouth who died at sea during two world wars. The striking memorial, easily distinguishable from the sea, is identical to two others at Plymouth and Chatham and records the names of 9,666 men and women who were lost in World War I and 14,922 who died in World War II, as well as the actions in which they were engaged. A database of these records is available online at www.memorials. inportsmouth.co.uk.

The **Blue Reef Aquarium** houses displays that simulate various underwater habitats and hold creatures associated with both local waters and the tropical species of more distant marine environments. At its centre is the Sea of Cortez, which is a large coral reef display, while other typical themes include Otter Holt, the Solent coastline and Warmer Waters, together with an extensive ocean display that has an underwater tunnel.

The **D-Day Museum** opened in 1984 to mark the 40th anniversary of D-Day and is the only museum in the United Kingdom devoted exclusively to the story of the Normandy Landings. Portsmouth and the local area played a major part in the preparations, assembly and deployment of the forces, with the Solent and its adjacent harbours filled with most of the Allied fleet.

This museum includes the remarkable Overlord Embroidery commissioned by Lord Dulverton of Batsford (1915–92) as a memorial to all those who took part in Operation Overlord. It measures 272 feet (83m), has 34 panels and is the largest object of its kind in the world, with a commentary to explain the themes and details. There are also extensive displays about the various aspects of the huge amphibious operations and the landings in Normandy, including items of uniform and equipment, documents and other mementoes, as well as a range of specialised vehicles, such as a Beach Armoured Recovery Vehicle, an LCVP (Landing Craft, Vehicle and Personnel, or 'Higgins Boat') and a Churchill tank converted to a Crocodile flamethrower. Other displays about the Portsmouth area in 1942 to 1944 cover naval preparations, the assembly of land forces before embarkation and the role of civilians. The experience is enhanced by a moving film show, comprising original, historic and archive material and available in a number of languages.

The Pyramids is an indoor leisure and swimming facility, with wave, tropical leisure and toddler pools, as well as flume rides and a café/bar.

At 1,950ft (591m), Southsea's **South Parade Pier** was originally built for passengers travelling to and from the Isle of Wight in 1879, but was destroyed by fire in 1904. Rebuilt and re-opened in 1908 at a reduced length of 600ft (183m), the new pier, unusually constructed with a concrete deck, was primarily a pleasure and promenading platform. It had two pavilions, the largest housing a 1,200-seat theatre and dance hall, as well as, at the seaward end, another hosting a bar and lounge.

A fire in 1967 severely damaged the theatre beyond repair and another conflagration, in 1974 during the filming of the rock-opera *Tommy*, destroyed the rest of the largest pavilion. This landward pavilion was rebuilt at a cost of £500,000 and now houses several show-bars alongside the familiar rainy day seaside amusements.

The Canoe Lake lies at the centre of the Great Morass that used to cover the area to the north-east of Southsea Castle, but was drained in the 19th century. It is used for sailing model boats and boating. Nearby is the abandoned Lumps Fort, built between 1859 and 1869, which is now a Rose Garden, containing a memorial to the Cockleshell Heroes. Other facilities include grass and hard tennis courts, bowling greens, putting (both pitch and putt and more basic varieties) and a Model Village.

Located just behind the Canoe Lake, an accessible, unusual **Natural History Museum** shows in detail the range of wildlife that inhabits the marshlands, woods and urban spaces of the local area. There is an extensive Victorian Museum collection, as well as topical exhibitions about geology and dinosaurs, while all visitors will enjoy the aquarium and butterfly house.

About a mile (1.5km) further along the seafront, the **Royal Marines Museum** is housed in the officers' mess of the barracks that were constructed to house the Royal Marine Artillery (RMA) at Eastney between 1862 and 1867. In 1923, the RMA amalgamated with the Royal Marine Light Infantry (RMLI) and became the home of the Portsmouth Division of the Royal Marines. The barracks themselves have been converted into houses and apartments, but the museum provides a fascinating insight into the history and fighting culture of these sea soldiers since their founding as part of the Royal Navy in 1664. There are also exhibitions devoted to operations in the Falklands War and in various locations around the world in more recent times, including Iraq and Afghanistan.

Portsmouth City Centre

The centre of Portsmouth has suffered from the unfortunate effects of German bombing in World War II, a hasty rebuilding and development programme in the 1950s and 1960s and the persistence of a range of hideous modern residential and corporate building experiments. The most notorious example, the Tricorn Centre, a 1960s concrete monstrosity that combined car parks, shops and residences was voted the most hated building in Britain by Radio 4 listeners in 2001 and was demolished in 2004. Much of the centre's skyline is dominated today by the modernist buildings of the expanded University of Portsmouth and the distant prospect of high-rise developments at Gunwharf Quays.

The Commercial Road shopping precinct caters for just about every consumer requirement and has an extensive, well-stocked shopping centre, the Cascades, and numerous street market

Worth a Look

Portsmouth Guildhall was built and formally opened in 1890, but in January 1941, the whole interior was destroyed by a German incendiary bomb. It was restored, with several new facilities and a concert theatre.

Behind the Guildhall, **Victoria Park** offers a surprisingly refreshing break from the bustle of the city. There are numerous naval memorials and a central enclosure that contains a variety of birds and small mammals, including guinea pigs and rabbits.

Just across the road on the far side of the park is the **Roman Catholic Cathedral** of St John the Evangelist, founded in 1882 and built in the Romanesque style.

A short walk from the shopping centre along Commercial Road, the **Charles Dickens Birthplace Museum** is in the house in which Dickens was born in 1812 and where he lived for the first few months of his life. The museum is one of a number of handsome brick houses preserved when the houses of the old Commercial Road were demolished in the 1960s to make way for wholesale road and residential development. The parlour, the dining room and the bedroom where Charles was born have been decorated and furnished in a style appropriate to the status of his parents, John and Elizabeth Dickens, in 1809. A small exhibition and a series of prints illustrate the works of Charles Dickens and some of his personal effects are on display, including the couch on which he died. The city features in *Nicholas Nickleby*, when the hero and Smike make their way to Portsmouth and join a theatrical troupe.

stalls. However, the shabby 'Sixties' appearance and faded amenities indicate that it is close to the point where serious regeneration is required.

Further Out

Farlington Marshes, to the northeast of the city, are home to a variety of sea, wading and migrating birds and provide an opportunity for a bracing circular walk of about two miles (3km) around a flat promontory that reaches into Langstone harbour.

Situated in the north of the harbour, just off the westbound M275, **Port Solent Marina** has a pleasant mix of boutique shops, reliable restaurants and a multi-screen cinema complex, all part of a modern marina and waterfront residential development. There is plenty of free parking and the opportunity to enjoy the nautical atmosphere away from the crowds.

Just to the west is **Portchester**, which before Portsmouth and Fareham took its trade, was a medieval borough that in 1294 had been given a market and fair by Edward I. It declined in importance as Portsmouth's more favourable position at the mouth of the harbour enabled quicker access across the Channel. Nowadays, the village of Portchester has been swallowed up by the surrounding residential develop-ment, but the lower part of Castle Street, nearest the castle, has retained its traditional charm, with several well-established and distinctive 18th- and 19th-century houses.

Portchester Castle should not be missed and is worth a significant detour. The original fort at Portchester, prob-ably known to the Romans as Portus Adurni, was one of a chain of fortifica-tions stretching from Norfolk through to Hampshire that was designed to protect the coast against raiders and pirates or act as a military outpost in an area where Saxons had already settled. However, it is also possible that Portchester was initially built by a commander of the Roman Channel fleet, Carausius, who set himself up as Emperor in Britain and Northern Gaul in the late third century, and then needed to defend Britain against the legitimate Emperor.

Whatever its origins, Portchester castle is the most complete example of Roman military architecture in Britain and is the only structure of its type standing to its full height (20ft/6m) in northern Europe. The unbroken square circuit of its walls encloses 9 acres (3.5ha) and 14 of its original 20 bastions are still standing, from which the fort would have been defended by stone- and bolt-throwing Roman artillery called *ballistae*. At some stage in the early Saxon period, the fort appears to have been occupied by Germanic mercenar-ies, but later the walls enclosed a civilian settlement, which became a fortified *burh* (origin of the word *borough*) under Alfred the Great and his successors as part of a systematic scheme to defend Wessex against the Danes.

After the Norman Conquest, the possibilities of the fort were appreci-ated by William Mauduit, its new owner, and a castle was built in the north-west corner in about 1080 by digging a moat and initially building a wooden stockade. William Pont de L'Arche, a subsequent owner, replaced this basic arrangement in about 1130 with a massive two-storey stone keep and a masonry curtain wall, with the old circuit of the Roman fort walls being utilised as an outer bailey. At the same time, he also founded an Augus-tinian priory in the opposite corner and its church remained, even after the monks found it impossible to co-exist with the military garrison and moved to Southwick some 20 years later in the reign of King Stephen. By 1158, the castle had reverted to the Crown and, in about 1180, the keep was sig-nificantly heightened under Henry II and further accommodation was built around the inside of the curtain wall, reflecting the frequency of its use, both as a royal place of embarkation and as a convenient place from which to hunt in the Forest of Bere, to the north.

During the Hundred Years War, Portchester became increasingly im-portant both as a staging post for expeditions to France and in repelling cross-Channel raids, and the defences were regularly modernised. Most of the domestic buildings within the castle that can be seen today date from the reign of Richard II, who from 1396 built a palace and upgraded the defen-sive arrangements and accommodation. Not long after, Henry V used the castle as an assembly and embarkation point

St Mary's Church, Portchester

St Mary's Church within the castle was built for the Augustinian priory around 1130 and is an outstanding example of a Norman Romanesque church. It has a cruciform plan, with a nave, chancel, transepts, central tower, and north chapel. Although the chancel has been shortened, the south transept has been removed and some restoration is evident, the church retains its original Norman character and features.

The really compelling feature is its west door arch which has several bands of zig-zag mouldings and floral designs, as well as roundels that have the zodiacal signs of Pisces and Sagittarius. The shafts have incised spiral and V decoration and the central window above is accompanied by two smaller blank arches decorated with quatrefoils within; and all are framed by zig-zag mouldings. The same delicate yet expressive decoration is repeated in the arches and capitals of the tower crossing, which have scallop and fluted patterns, as well as in the arcading of the chancel and the north transept. Other details worth noting are the 12th-century font, with its intersecting arches and vine decoration and the arms of Elizabeth I (1577) and Queen Anne (1710). An alabaster bust of Sir Thomas Cornwallis (1618) keeps its own company in a church remarkably and pleasantly devoid of overt memorials.

Outside, there is very little trace of the rest of the priory, which has long been absorbed into the graveyard, apart from an uneven pattern of masonry where the west range joined the church and the garderobe chutes of the reredorter (best seen from outside the castle) pierced the old Roman walls.

for the Agincourt expedition in 1415 and his subsequent campaigns. Under Henry VIII, a very large storehouse was built in the outer bailey, which was later

Worth a Look

Behind Portsdown Hill the small village of **Boarhunt** has a delightful 11th-century Saxon church, which, although restored and gaining a gallery in 1853, retains its original character and features, including Saxon windows and distinctive stone decoration. There are also later box pews and a three-decker pulpit.

demolished, and other modifications were made to the castle's accommodation in the time of Elizabeth I and her wars with Spain. Thereafter, it saw little action, but was used regularly to store munitions and house troops, notably during the Civil War. From the Seven Years War (1756–63) onwards, it was a detention camp for thousands of Dutch, French, Spanish and American prisoners, particularly during the Napoleonic Wars and the Anglo–American War of 1812–14. Those who died in captivity were usually deposited in the tidal mud-flats to the south of the castle.

This excellent and fascinating desti-

Royal Marines Museum

nation is well served by an exhibition in the keep, which clearly explains the history of the castle and displays finds that have been excavated on the site. A good audio tour is available and there is a superb view from the roof of the keep. A stroll around the walls is strongly recommended and, for children, hide-and-seek in the medieval part of the castle is always popular.

On Portsdown Hill one of 'Palmerston's Follies', **Fort Nelson** is a restored Victorian artillery fort overlooking Portsmouth Harbour, with over 19 acres of grass ramparts, underground chambers and military buildings to examine and explore, including the Officers' Mess, the underground magazine and the gun batteries. The Fort is home to the Royal Armouries national artillery collection with over 350 historic guns and cannons on display, as well as a café and gift shop. Particular favourites are the Great Turkish Bombard of 1464, used in the Dardanelles, Saddam Hussein's 'Supergun', the (rather anachronistic) trebuchet from the feature film '*Gladiator*' and Mallet's Mortar, one of

three items featuring in the Guinness Book of Records. There are daily gun firings, re-enactments and special events throughout the year. A short walk away is a monument to Lord Nelson, erected and paid for by those who served with him during his naval career.

Just two miles north of Portsdown Hill, on the road to Wickham, **Southwick** repays a visit because of the

Charles Dickens House

Southwick

uniqueness of its situation and the unspoiled character of its houses and community. The village is unusual because it is almost wholly owned by the Southwick Estate and all estate houses have dark-red-painted front doors and restrictive covenants as part of the tenancy agreements. Its church is an ecclesiastical 'peculiar', meaning that the local landowner has the right to nominate the clergy.

Southwick was the birthplace of

Great View

To the north of the city **Portsdown Hill** is possibly the most remarkable view in the county. The chalk ridge, which runs from Bedhampton almost to Fareham, has several viewpoints with car parks and the visitor will be rewarded, particularly on a fine day, with extensive vistas of the city, the Solent, the Isle of Wight and much else, including Chichester and the South Downs in the east and the New Forest to the west. Access can be gained from Portsdown Hill Road and there is ample parking and grassy recreational land. Despite the scarring caused by quarrying and extensive residential development, part of the hill has been designated a Site of Special Scientific Interest, owing to its insect and small mammal habitats, and the back of the hill to the west of the A3 falls away onto gently sloping farmland as far as Southwick and the Forest of Bere, offering good walking opportunities. The crest of the hill is pierced at one-mile intervals by the Palmerston forts, built in the 1860s to defend Portsmouth from possible attack from a French army landing nearby, occupying Portsdown Hill and deploying rifled guns to bombard the Dockyard.

Bishop William of Wykeham, eminent statesman and local boy made good in the 14th century and the founder of Winchester College and New College, Oxford. It is also the site of Southwick Priory, which was founded in the 12th century by monks who moved from Portchester Castle as the fortress grew in size, importance and, presumably, distractions. Only fragments of the priory remain, adjacent to a green on the golf course. After its dissolution, the estate was granted to John Whyte, a follower of the Earl of Southampton, who demolished the priory and built a manor house that was subsequently owned by the Nortons, the most famous of whom was a Parliamentary colonel in the Civil War, who distinguished himself at the Battle of Cheriton and other actions. The house was gutted by fire in 1838, but was restored by 1841, only to be requisitioned, along with the estate, during World War II, when it was General Eisenhower's headquarters for the D-Day landings in 1944. After the war, it became *HMS Dryad*, a training establishment for the officers and ratings of the Royal Navy, specialising in warfare and operations. More recently, the Royal Navy has consolidated its warfare training at *HMS Collingwood* and the site is now occupied by the Defence Police College.

Southwick has two good public houses, The Red Lion and The Golden Lion, next to the restored and functioning Southwick Brewhouse.

To the North-West

Fareham is a bustling borough at the north-west point of Portsmouth Harbour, which is the main entry and

> ### Worth a Look
>
> The **Westbury Manor Museum**, an 18th-century Grade II listed building with formal Victorian style gardens, displays themed exhibitions about local crafts, industries and social history.

exit point for Gosport. In the past, it had been a thriving port and famous for its clay soil, from which bricks, tiles and chimney pots were manufactured, notably the 'Fareham red bricks' that were used in the construction of the Royal Albert Hall in London. Now a largely retail, residential and light industry centre, it has a very attractive but somewhat detached High Street (away from the main shopping centre) with fine Georgian houses built with the local bricks.

Across The Harbour

Originally a fishing village in the Middle Ages, **Gosport** was used by Parliamentary forces in the Civil War to bombard Portsmouth. Starting with a town wall and moat under Charles II, the town progressively became part of the massive fortifications that surrounded the harbour and Dockyard. It very rapidly became overspill accommodation for those who worked in the Dockyard or provided services to the Navy. An 18th-century commentator was less than complimentary when he wrote about the 'narrowness and slander of a small country town without its rural simplicity and with a full share of the vice of Portsmouth, polluted by

Gosport Museums

The Gosport side of the harbour entrance is dominated by Fort Blockhouse. The site was first fortified with a wooden tower, but Henry VIII built an eight-gun battery there in 1539. The fort was more heavily fortified over the centuries until it largely reached its current configuration in 1845. In 1904, it became, as *HMS Dolphin*, the Portsmouth base for the Royal Navy's submarines, but, after the withdrawal of the last diesel-electric submarines from the Royal Navy, the base was closed in 1999. Today, the **Royal Navy Submarine Museum** occupies part of HMS Dolphin. Still visible is the tall tower that contains the Submarine Escape Training Tank, a 100-foot (30m) deep container of water used to instruct all Royal Navy submariners in pressurised escape, which opened in 1954.

The **museum** represents a unique and fascinating insight into the peculiar lives of submariners in peace and war, with a wealth of interesting detail and a great many exhibits on display. On site are some real submarines, one of which, *HMS Alliance*, has been sited on dry land so that visitors can walk through and experience the sensations, smells and sounds of being in an operational submarine underwater. Also on display is *Holland 1*, the Royal Navy's first ever operational submarine in 1901, which was recovered from the seabed, and a miniature X-craft used for underwater attacks on ships and harbours, as well as a modern submersible and a 'one-man' German midget submarine from World War II. All in all, it is well worth the trip across the harbour and children are sure to like it.

Part of the family of Portsmouth's naval museums, **Explosion! The Museum of Naval Firepower** is an unusual attraction – an (inert!) atomic bomb greets visitors on arrival – housed within the 18th-century buildings of the Royal Navy's former armaments depot of Priddy's Hard. The former storehouses contain an impressive and absorbing inventory of devices and weapons that were designed to go bang at sea, including cannon and guns, shells and munitions, mines, torpedoes and modern missiles. These are brought to life through imaginative audio-visual effects, computer interactive displays and hands-on opportunities. In addition, there are exhibitions devoted to life at the armaments depot over the years of its existence and to the people who worked there.

Both **Explosion!** and the **Royal Navy Submarine Museum** can be reached by taking the Gosport ferry (4 minutes' transit) to the Millennium Promenade. On arrival, a Millennium Trail guides walkers northwards to Explosion! (20 minutes' walk), or south across Haslar Bridge to the Submarine Museum (10 minutes). The whole two-mile (3km) Millennium Trail, for which a pamphlet describing a number of interesting buildings and sites is available, takes about one hour to cover on foot. Alternatively, taxis can be hired at the Millennium Promenade.

Worth a Look

The more adventurous visitors and those who come to the Gosport peninsula by car will easily be able to venture further afield to Stokes Bay and Lee-on-the-Solent.

Stokes Bay is part of a long continuous shingle beach, which stretches from Lee-on-the-Solent to the Harbour Entrance. The foreshore and the open wild grounds at Browndown and Gilkicker, designated a Site of Special Scientific Interest, sustain a diversity of wildlife. There are spectacular views over the Solent and to the Isle of Wight and the coast is especially good for invigorating walking.

Lee-on-the-Solent tried to develop as a fashionable late Victorian seaside resort, boosted by the extension of the railway in 1894 and the construction of a pier, but never prospered. Its station is now an amusement arcade. However, with a good beach, a promenade and great views out into the Solent and to the Isle of Wight, the resort still attracts plenty of tourists. It has an interesting memorial to Fleet Air Arm personnel and, in hangars on the former *HMS Daedalus* Fleet Air Arm base, an outstanding museum collection of over 60 hovercraft, ranging in size from the very large to the very small. There are no formal opening times, but people can contact the museum in advance to arrange a visit on enquiries@hovercraft-museum.org and there is an annual Hovershow, which normally occurs in the last week in July (see www.hovercraft-museum.org).

Fort Brockhurst is one of five forts known as the Gosport Advanced Lines, built between 1858 and 1862 to defend Portsmouth Harbour from an attack by troops that had landed on the Gosport side. It was designed to house 308 men and 73 guns. It was acquired by English Heritage and is used as a museum for items from the reserve collection, with workshops and a training facility. It is only open to the public on the second Saturday of every month between March and October (11 am until 3 pm).

the fortunes of sailors and the extravagances of harlots'. However, Gosport prospered and grew in line with the growth of Britain's maritime power, especially in periods of tension and war and much of the land was owned and used by the Army and Navy, right up to the modern era.

Until the late 19th century, its administrative and commercial centre had been the village of Alverstoke and its seafront at Stokes Bay, some 2 miles (3km) inland from the harbour. This village retained its rural character well into the 20th century and keeps its status as a more upmarket residential area today, as some of the older houses demonstrate. There had been plans in the early 19th century to make Alverstoke a major seaside resort, with

Gosport's Lost Railways

A railway line was proposed to Gosport in 1834 because of the intense rivalry between Portsmouth and Southampton. Portsmouth citizens objected to the inclusion of Southampton in the proposed London and Southampton Railway Company and would not allow a main line to run into Portsmouth. Nor would the military authorities permit the breaching of the military fortifications at Hilsea Lines, which defended the northern shore of Portsea Island. In the end, the London and South Western Railway took over the project and, as the fortifications of Gosport were close to the town centre, the railway was able to approach almost to the centre, while at the same time servicing the Royal Clarence Yard victualling and supply base.

The line consequently opened in 1841 and, on the completion of Osborne House on the Isle of Wight, was extended within the ramparts to allow the Royal family to travel to the Royal Victoria Station, which remains today. However, general traffic was badly affected by the opening of a direct service from London to Portsmouth in 1847. From 1863 to 1915, a branch line was opened to Stokes Bay where it joined up with a ferry link to Ryde on the Isle of Wight. Another branch line ran from 1894 to Lee-on-the-Solent in an attempt to stimulate holiday traffic, but closed to passengers in 1931 and to freight in 1935.

From 1914, the major user of the railway to Gosport was the War Department, with heavy traffic to the Royal Clarence Yard and neighbouring armaments depots, as well as in support of troop movements and in transporting wounded servicemen to and from Haslar Hospital. Activity was again very busy during the Second World War, but in March 1941 the Royal Victoria Station received a direct hit from an incendiary bomb which caused the roof to collapse. After the war and with demobilisation, the line's utility diminished and the line closed to passengers in June 1953 and to freight in January 1969. The station is now derelict, but the line to Royal Clarence yard is being restored.

bathing facilities, an extension to the railway from Fareham and a racecourse, as well as a pier at Stokes Bay. Despite the provision of a floating bridge from the Point in Portsmouth and the building of the railway extension in 1863, the scheme never attracted the necessary interest and investment. A solitary reminder of that era and its aspirations is the impressive terrace of nineteen houses in Crescent Road dating from 1826.

Over the centuries, Gosport has grown in size and importance in parallel with Portsmouth, mainly as the site for numerous fortifications and defence, mainly naval, training and technical establishments, and today it is overlaid by a densely settled residential area. It can be accessed by foot passengers via the ferry that crosses frequently from Portsmouth Harbour station or by road (the long way round) via the M275 and Fareham. Its post-war development has meant that there are very few reasons to tempt the visitor onto the Gosport peninsula by road, as the traffic is often heavy and the effort rarely worth the bother. Surprisingly, there is no longer a rail connection. However, the very worthwhile attractions that do exist in Gosport can usually be reached by taking the passenger ferry from just outside Portsmouth Harbour station. This short passage and a stroll along the Gosport side give a first-class view up harbour and the experience is thoroughly recommended.

Further west and three miles (5km) inland from the mouth of the River Meon in the middle of water meadows and woods, the tidy, prosperous village of **Titchfield** was a thriving port and market town in the Middle Ages, but succumbed to silting. Its haven, drained in the 17th century, where the river flows into the Solent, is an attractive area for wildlife and walking. Nearby, hidden by a bridge, with the remains of a sea-lock at its south end, is the second oldest canal in England (after Exeter), completed in 1611 and intended to offset the effects of silting and to irrigate the water meadows on both sides.

As a result of the canal's construction, the outfall of the River Meon to the sea was blocked, creating the wetlands that now form Titchfield Haven, National Nature Reserve (NNR). There is an enjoyable circular walk down to the sea and back again of about 6 miles

(10km), although the footpaths do tend to become muddy after and during wet weather.

The wide streets of the village contain Georgian houses, as well as others with timber and plaster construction, amid modern sympathetic development. The church (St Peter's), with evident Saxon and Norman origins, has several noteworthy features, including a striking Norman west doorway, 15th-century arcading and the imposing tombs of successive generations of Wriothesleys, earls of Southampton.

Titchfield Abbey was founded in 1222, as a minor house for Premonstratensian canons, an austere order of priests who were famous for their extensive scholarship and, at Titchfield, their library of 224 precious volumes. Its church was the site of the marriage of Henry VI to Margaret of Anjou in 1449. Dissolved in 1537 under Henry VIII, it was converted into a mansion called Place House by Thomas Wriothesley, the influential courtier and first earl of Southampton. An imposing towered gatehouse was built across the nave of the abbey church and the conventual buildings were adapted for secular use.

At the end of the 16th century, Place House was a refuge away from court for Henry Wriothesley, the third earl, who had offended Queen Elizabeth I following an intrigue with one her ladies and by involvement in the Essex rebellion. He was the patron and devoted friend of William Shakespeare and there is strong circumstantial evidence that Shakespeare shared part of his benefactor's internal exile at Titchfield while he awaited reprieve. A father and son surnamed Gobbo lived at Titchfield at

Worth a Look

A 13-mile (21km) section of the **Solent Way** can be walked between **Warsash** and the entrance to Portsmouth Harbour, giving panoramic views of the Solent and the Isle of Wight, without once getting your feet wet underfoot (unless you want to!).

A ferry is available in summer to cross the river to **Warsash**, which, once a thriving ship and boat building centre, now substantially caters to the yacht and leisure trade. It also home to Warsash Maritime Academy, which trains students for professions at sea.

about the right time, three years before the characters made famous in *The Merchant of Venice* first appeared on the stage (1596).

In 1781, Place House was partially demolished to create a romantic ruin and several local houses contain stones and decorative features from the abbey; the Bugle Hotel has a large salvaged fireplace. Today, visitors can still see the unusual nave and gatehouse, with their Tudor mullioned windows and chimneys and mostly standing to their full height, along with the foundations of the abbey buildings and several walls. Admission is free.

The **River Hamble** rises near Bishop's Waltham and flows for about 7.5 miles (12 km) before reaching Southampton Water between Warsash and Hamble-le-Rice. It is tidal for almost half its length and navigable in its lower reaches (below Botley), which,

together with plentiful supplies of local timber, has made the river a centre for shipbuilding since the Middle Ages. For most of the medieval period, royal ships were berthed and maintained in the river and Henry V's great warship the *Grace Dieu* sank in the river after a disastrous fire. Its wreck has been identified through archaeological excavation and its remains can be seen at very low tides.

A passenger ferry crosses the river between Hamble-le-Rice and Warsash, linking sections of the Solent Way and

Worth a Look

The Jolly Sailor is a pub of 18th-century origin that basks in the reflected glory of its role in the TV series *Howards' Way*, but is, for all that, a very pleasant location on the waterfront.

Bursledon Brickworks is the only surviving example of a traditional steam-powered brickworks in the country, with exhibits and machinery on display. It is open only on Thursdays between 10 am and 4 pm.

Bursledon Windmill, built in 1813–14, is still in working order. This five-storey tower mill replaced a predecessor of 1766 and remained in commercial use until the 1880s. The restored wooden machinery is in perfect working order and milling takes place whenever the sails can turn in the wind. Visitor facilities are available in a re-erected 17th-century barn.

E9 European Coastal Path. The river is also home to several large marinas, notably Port Hamble Marina, and various boatyards, on both banks as far upstream as Bursledon.

The upper reaches of the river are delightful, with pleasant walks to be had in the vicinity of **Manor Farm Country Park**, where one can walk through Dock Copse and Foster's Copse.

Opened in 1984, Manor Farm, with its original 15th-century hall and the neighbouring 13th-century church of St Bartholomew, dates from medieval times, but has been progressively updated over the centuries. The various outbuildings date from the 16th century and in some cases have been re-erected after removal from their original locations elsewhere in Hampshire.

The park itself comprises 400 acres (160ha) of arable farmland, grassland and ancient woodland, together with riverside habitats, salt marshes and freshwater ponds, all of which can be easily accessed by a network of trails. Over 150 acres (60ha) of the park's woodland, with its oak, ash, wild cherry and lime trees, have been designated a Site of Special Scientific Interest. The favourable habitats encourage a variety of flora and fauna, depending on the time of year, with most native and transiting woodland birds, including chiffchaffs, woodpeckers and nightingales, in evidence. Also, along the river, the usual waders can be seen, along with cormorants, wildfowl, gulls and herons, while the hedgerows support yellowhammers, hedge sparrows and bullfinches.

Trails and facilities also exist for cycling and riding. A detailed park map and brochure, including walking trails and points of interest, are available at the farm. In addition to the Pantry Tea Rooms, there are three children's play areas and plenty of sites for picnics.

An important maritime focus for some time, both for its shipbuilding and reputation as a safe anchorage, the **Hamble** estuary is home to over 3,500 leisure craft and yachts. The narrow streets of **Hamble-le-Rice** contain a variety of picturesque houses, boutiques and shops, all of which are caught up in the activities centred on one of the country's leading yachting centres. In summer, the streets, the river and the waterfront are very crowded, but the genial atmosphere and opportunities to watch all the activity are genuinely enjoyable, once you can park.

The remains of an Iron Age bank and ditch are visible on the foreshore and the village had a priory in the Middle Ages, whose foundations were discovered in the vicinity of the 12th-century church (St Andrew's) and whose chapel forms the chancel today. The church is definitely worth a look for its mixture of Norman, Early English and Perpendicular features and for the interior details of its impressive roof.

In the medieval and Tudor periods, Hamble was still considered to be a secure haven for large ships and its continuing importance is indicated by the existence of St Andrew's Castle (a Henry VIII coastal fortlet, built around 1545, but now disappeared into the sea) and a Victorian gun emplacement.

During World War II, two now abandoned airfields nearby were training centres for aircrew learning to fly Spitfire, Lancaster and Wellington aircraft. Also, through a pipeline under Southampton Water from the Fawley oil refinery, a fuel terminal at Hamble supplied the Pipe Line under the Ocean (PLUTO), which, in turn, provided fuel for the D-Day landings. PLUTO itself started at Sandown on the Isle of Wight, but was supplied by tankers loading at the Hamble terminal.

British visitors of a certain age will recall that the village and its river, together with the upriver village of Bursledon, were recognisable locations in the 1980s BBC Television series Howards' Way.

Bursledon has a shipbuilding tradition dating back to the medieval period and many medieval and early Tudor warships were built in the vicinity, taking advantage of the gently sloping river banks and the ready availability of timber. During the 18th and 19th centuries, very large warships were constructed, including *HMS Elephant* (1786), which would be Nelson's flagship at the Battle of Copenhagen. Although by the 1870s, with the introduction of steam-powered iron and steel ships, the construction of large wooden ships declined, the building, repair and maintenance of smaller vessels continues in a variety of yards and businesses.

To the North-East

To the north and east of Portsmouth, much of the countryside is either open farmland or heath and bracken-covered chalk downland that is interspersed with softly wooded, well-watered valleys. On the western side of the A3 road, the most distinctive features are the hangers (from the Anglo-Saxon *hangar*, meaning 'sloping wood') – comprising mostly beech woods that cling to the sides of steep chalk escarpments.

Just off the Portsmouth to Petersfield trunk road, **Queen Elizabeth Country Park** is a 1,400-acre (565ha) park – spread over three hills; two wooded and one open downland – and offers parking and facilities to enable visitors and families to enjoy woodland walks, waymarked paths and cycle trails of varying difficulty and distance. Both War Down (wooded) and Butser Hill (open down) can be reached by car, but the park never seems crowded and there is plenty to excite and entertain even children along the way. The careful balance struck between conservation and access means that a wide assortment of flora and animals find a congenial habitat in the park. Familiar small mammals, as well as rabbits, squirrels, foxes and badgers, are frequently sighted, together with roe deer and bats.

At 889 feet (271m), **Butser Hill** is the highest point on the South Downs and the second highest in the county. The views over Hampshire and West Sussex are worth the climb alone, although the ridge behind can be accessed by car. Scattered around the hill is evidence of prehistoric settlement, in the form of ancient defensive earthworks, field boundaries and strip lynchets. Numerous Neolithic and Bronze Age artefacts have been found by field walkers and archaeologists in the past.

At **Butser Ancient Farm,** an innovative project is both a visitor attraction and an experimental archaeology scheme that graphically demonstrates and investigates life in the Iron Age

(1000BC to 43BC) and the Roman era in Britain. Everything is made as far as possible with materials, tools and resources that were available at the time and there are demonstrations of Iron Age industrial and agricultural techniques. Authentic replica tools are used and even early breeds of domestic animals are roped in to help with the recreation. A huge wood and thatch roundhouse of the period, earthworks and other building representations can be examined at close quarters.

Just to the north and off the beaten track, the pretty village of **Buriton** used to be the point where coaches stopped on the Portsmouth Road ahead of their steep ascent over the chalk hills in the days before the cutting through the saddle east of Butser was excavated (by French prisoners). The grouping of the village pond, nearby church and manor house is quintessentially English. The church has a variety of interesting Norman and Early English features, while the manor house was once owned by the father of Edward Gibbon, the historian and author of *The Decline and Fall of the Roman Empire*. The writer grew up here, served as a captain in the Hampshire Militia and lived at the manor house until the death of his father, when he moved to London.

Situated on a spur of chalk downland nearby, just off the A3, **Chalton** is a peaceful, settled village and a first-class base for a range of walks to the south and east of Petersfield and along the Sussex border. It has a popular thatched public house, the Red Lion, dating from the 15th century, and a church with a range of Early English and later medieval features.

Just to the south and standing alone in a field, which used to be a clearing in the Forest of Bere, the chapel of St Hubert at **Idsworth** was abandoned in the 19th century and escaped the obligatory 'makeover' so prevalent in churches at the time. Possibly dating from Saxon times, but mainly Norman in appearance and with a small 18th-century bell tower, this exquisite little building still retains its 18th-century gallery, pulpit and pews. However, its claim to fame and eminence rests on a series of early 14th-century wall paintings depicting the life of St Hubert, with (appropriately) lively hunting scenes, and the familiar story of St John the Baptist. Underneath are graffiti that are in fact cues for new benedictions that had to be said by the priest after the issue of new services in 1481, presumably before he received the necessary breviary.

The market town of **Petersfield** is situated on the northern slopes of the South Downs and is unique in being wholly within an Area of Outstanding Natural Beauty, soon to be part of the South Downs National Park.

The town was founded during the 12th century by William Fitz Robert, 2nd Earl of Gloucester and grew in prosperity, owing to its position on frequently travelled routes, local sheep farming and cottage industry manufacturing of leather and cloth. The town had markets for sheep, horse and cattle trading and three annual fairs. Its church (St Peter's) is Norman in origin, but was severely handled by Victorian restorers, although it has a host of surviving features that will interest the discerning visitor. Today, Petersfield's market square holds regular markets throughout the week, as well as monthly Farmers' and French markets. The square has an equestrian statue of King William III (of Orange), which was financed and raised by a local admirer long after the king had died. This is the only statue of William in a town square in the United Kingdom outside Northern Ireland and, as such, attracts bands of marching Orangemen in mid-July, anxious to commemorate William's victory at the Battle of the Boyne.

Apart from its agreeable market town atmosphere and amenities, Petersfield is an excellent base for forays into the open downland, the extensive network of paths and bridleways and quiet villages to the east that border West Sussex. It also has a particularly well-stocked second-hand bookshop and, to the east, a heath and lake which make for a pleasant stroll, as well as a cluster of 21 Bronze Age barrows.

Although **Selborne**'s main road is used as a 'rat-run' for traffic heading to and from the M3, this charming, traditional Hampshire village lying at the foot of steep, wooded slopes retains its character and dignity. It is famous as the birthplace, home and burial site of the Reverend Gilbert White, the 18th-century pioneering exponent of natural history and author of *The Natural History and Antiquities of Selborne*, which was published in 1789. His house, The Wakes, is now a well-presented and fascinating museum and memorial library devoted to his life and work, with a separate section that recalls the careers of two explorers of the Oates family. Captain Lawrence Oates died with Captain Scott on his last Antarctic expedition of 1911–12 and is remembered for his last words, 'I am just going outside and may be some time.' His uncle, Frank Oates, who died on an expedition in Africa, is the other person commemorated. Also of note are the finds excavated from the site of the nearby Augustinian Priory that was founded in 1232 and suppressed in 1484, which include medieval alembics (chemical distilling devices).

A commentator on White's *Natural History* wrote, 'Open the book where you will, it takes you out of doors.' Selborne is an excellent place from which to walk and there are several well-marked, very pleasant paths up into the hangers and to the site of the former priory, a mile or so to the east. Behind The Wakes and its garden is Selborne Hanger, a wooded hill owned by the National Trust, where White recorded most of his observations about the local wildlife and habitats. Visitors can take the Zig-Zag Path to the top, where a monolith known as the Wishing Stone can be found.

The village itself contains a number of stone cottages and a green, known as the Plestor, as well as Gracious Street, which leads to an old smithy, Wheelwright's, and the former workhouse, Fisher's Buildings. The Norman church, much of it rebuilt in the 19th century, has a churchyard which holds the grave of Gilbert White. A memorial window to White in the church depicts St Francis of Assisi preaching to 82 birds, all of which are to be found in the *Natural History*.

From Roman times until the Industrial Revolution in the 18th century, **Bramshott** was the centre for the

Butser Ancient Farm

Petersfield Market

mining and smelting of iron ore from the Weald. Much of the woodland was felled to produce charcoal and depressions in the local landscape are the remains of iron ore quarries. The hammer mills were powered by the force of water channelled through various ponds and waterfalls, the remains of which can be seen at nearby Waggoners Wells (formerly Wakener's Wells). The last mill, built in the 17th century, was operating until 1924, producing paper for the manufacture of postal orders. Three of the original ponds, the subject of a poem by Tennyson in 1860, can be found in a 640

Worth a Visit

Nearby, at Holt Pound (actually in Surrey), **Birdworld** is home to over 1,000 birds and is one of the most comprehensive attractions of its kind in the country. There are 26 acres (10ha) of parkland and landscaped gardens, housing birds from around the world, Underwater World (with baby alligators) and the Jenny Wren Farm (with 'animal encounter' opportunities), all of which are popular with children.

Just before Hampshire becomes Surrey at Liphook, the family-friendly **Hollycombe Steam Collection** displays and operates a variety of heritage steam-powered attractions. At its heart, it has a Victorian and Edwardian Fairground where both gentle and embryonic white-knuckle rides compete for the attention of both young and old. There are three enjoyable steam railways, as well as traction engines, period farming exhibits and domestic animals, all set in highly attractive gardens and with spectacular views to the south.

acre (260ha) area of commons and woodland owned by the National Trust which is ideal for walking and exploring.

Although systematically forested as late as Norman times, the area of **Alice Holt Forest** was, in the Roman era, a centre for the production of red and black Samian ware and a great deal of pottery and evidence of industrial oc-cupation has been found in the local area. Owned by the Forestry Commission, which has a research station there, the forest covers six square miles (15 sq km) and most of the oaks were planted in 1812 to replace trees that had been taken for the construction of Royal Navy ships. Now the oaks have been joined by larch, firs and pines and every year about 25 acres (10ha) are felled for commercial purposes and replanted (oaks when 120 to 150 years old, pines when 55 to 65). Today, the forest has lots of walks and five marked trails of about a mile in length on which a variety of native wildlife can usually be encountered, including roe deer.

To the East

The former market and manufacturing town of **Havant** has been swallowed up by the greater Portsmouth conurbation. It lies on the route of a Roman road that led from Chichester to Winchester. Because of its abundant springs, it used to be primarily engaged in parchment-making, tanning and cloth manufacture. At its centre are St Faith's church, which has an unusual Early English vaulted chancel, but is largely Victorian, and the oldest house in the town, the (appropriately named) Old House at Home, virtually next door in South Street, which dates from the 16th century.

To the south of Havant, **Langstone** used to be the port of Havant and ships used to berth at the quay until the 19th century. Some of the terraced houses in Langstone's High Street date back to the 18th century, with slots for wooden barriers on their door frames indicating how often the village has been flooded. The High Street used to give access to the Wade Way, a causeway that led across to Hayling Island at low tide since prehistoric times and before the channel was deepened as part of a 19th-century canal scheme.

The village used to have a level crossing and a station on the 'Hayling Billy' railway line from Havant, which ran, with holiday and farm traffic, from 1867 to 1964. The line has long since disappeared and the track bed has become a very accessible cycle and bridle path. The remains of the rail bridge can still be seen to the right of the road bridge onto the island.

With the shallow Langstone harbour

Worth a Look

Just on the left before the bridge (built in 1956), there is a car park that leads to two good, virtually adjacent pubs – the Ship and the Royal Oak – and a mill that is quite possibly the most photographed and painted building in Hampshire. The windmill tower dates from about 1730 and for most of its existence there was an adjacent water-driven mill as well. A coastal footpath leads to the mill and, beyond, to Warblington and Emsworth.

Worth a Look

St Mary's in South Hayling is a good example of a restored (1868) early 13th-century church, with many original and interesting features, including a rare late 12th-century font.

At the quieter end of the island, in North Hayling, is St Peter's, a predominantly 12th–13th-century church, with later medieval additions, that was the only building in the village to survive a disastrous fire in March 1757.

Back on the mainland, **Warblington Church**, dedicated to St Thomas of Canterbury, is tucked away down a country lane on the foreshore of Langstone harbour, just south of the Havant to Emsworth Road. It is one of the most evocative churches in the county and amply repays detailed examination and contemplation. With Saxon features and Roman tiles evident in the tower, the church, which until 1840 also served the community at Emsworth a mile and a quarter (2km) away, has a roof that slopes almost to the ground and a 15th-century wooden porch thought to be made from ship's timbers. Inside, the present chancel and vestry were built in the 13th century over the Saxon nave and chancel, in conjunction with the present nave with its arcading on both sides extending to the west. In the churchyard are two early 19th-century watchmen's huts, erected to prevent body-snatching, and some intriguing tombstones, including one showing a ship sinking in memory of William Palmer 'that lost his life and vessel going into Dublin' in 1759 and another with a representation of the loss of *HMS Torbay* by fire.

to the west and Chichester harbour to the east, the uniformly flat **Hayling Island** has a number of developed residential areas and is a popular holiday destination, whose human occupation can be traced back to prehistoric times. At the Conquest, the island was given to the monks of Jumièges, but their priory struggled to survive against the inundations of the sea and was finally abandoned in 1324–5. The smaller, relocated establishment was suppressed by Henry V in 1413.

With one of the best beaches in the county, Hayling Island's life as a tourist destination really took off in the 1930s and it remains popular today, not only with day-trippers and locals, but also with people who return year after year. The southern portion of the island is the most popular and there are several well-established holiday villages amid the established communities. On its southern coast, it has four miles (6km) of shingle beach, with long stretches of sand below the high water mark, from Eastoke Point at the south-west corner to Sinah Common at the western end, where there are extensive dunes. The three main beaches of the Island have won both the European Blue Flag and the Keep Britain Tidy Group Seaside Award Flag for cleanliness and management. Parts of the beaches are screened by groynes which prevent the erosion of the beach and act as shelters from the onshore sea breezes. Offshore, there are fine views to the Isle of Wight and of the activity in the eastern Solent.

Near the centre of the beach is 'Funland', an amusement park that has the familiar combination of seaside rides and coin-fed entertainments, including white-knuckle rides like the Klondike Roller Coaster, Tornado and Drop Ride, as well as traditional fairground rides and over 200 video games and slot machines. There are also crazy golf, tenpin bowling and a 'Kidz Kingdom'.

Nearby is a tall, solitary, stone-faced brick tower, the only remains of a once square castle, built between 1513 and 1526, which enclosed a large courtyard and had towers at each corner. The Cotton family held the castle for the King during the Civil War and once it was captured Parliament ordered its demolition, leaving the single gatehouse tower as a seamark to assist navigation.

Right on the border with Sussex, **Emsworth** is a tidy, bustling town on Chichester Harbour, with a thriving, vibrant community (see www.emsworthonline.co.uk), a year-round, intimate association with sailing and excellent views of the harbour and beyond. As well as the marina and sailing club, it retains its shipwrights and chandleries, but also attracts artists, naturalists and walkers. There is a museum (open at the weekends from Easter until November) and, in addition to nine pubs, a range of high-quality shops, restaurants and cafes.

Dating from Saxon times, Emsworth was a busy port throughout the Middle Ages and well into the 19th century, when it thrived on shipbuilding, boat-building and rope making, as well as the processing of grain in its tidal mills and the brewing of ales, to supply London and Portsmouth. The port also handled timber and coal and was known for its oyster beds.

Chichester Harbour is internationally

Langstone

important for its birds (mostly wild-fowl, waterfowl and seabirds) and for its coastal habitats, as part of an Area of Outstanding Natural Beauty (AONB) and as the country's seventh biggest salt marsh.

There are opportunities to stroll along the sea walls that surround the harbour and two mill ponds, as well a very pleasant stroll across the fields and along the shoreline to Langstone Bridge and back, taking in Warbling-ton Church (10th century onwards) and the remains of Warblington Castle.

Other short walks are detailed on www.emsworth.biz/walks, while, for the more strenuous, there are circular walks around Thorney Island (approximately 8 miles/13km) and the Chidham Peninsula (approx 5.5 miles/9km).

A Trip down the Meon Valley

The **River Meon** starts south of the village of East Meon, flows north, then north-west to West Meon and south-west to Warnford, before finally

The Meon Valley Railway Path

heading south to the Solent near Titch-field, to where, until the 17th century, it was navigable by coastal vessels. Its river valley, followed by the A32 road, is studded with neat, settled villages, prosperous agricultural communities and more than its fair share of interesting churches, most of which have their origins in the most obscure period of the Dark Ages. There are excellent opportunities for varied walks and tours by car in landscapes that combine easy access, rural tranquillity and impressive views of chalk downlands.

Set amid chalk hills in a winding valley, with the Meon rising just to the south and flowing through it, the attractive village of **East Meon** has picturesque old cottages and one of the finest churches, if not the best, in Hampshire, which well repays a careful exploration. The medieval Court House, a private residence today, with walls four feet thick, corbels of kings and bishops and original windows, is where the bishops of Winchester and their agents used to hear pleas, collect rents and dispense justice in this part of the diocese. Isaak Walton, the author of The Compleat Angler, used to fish on the banks of East Meon's trout stream.

There are opportunities for walks of varying length and difficulty in all directions over the surrounding chalk hills.

West Meon retains its pretty cottages and, away from the road, much of its

East Meon

East Meon Church

Backed by a steep, wooded hill, the church, with its thick walls, was built soon after the Norman Conquest and has a sturdy 12th-century tower, with characteristic zig-zag patterns around the windows and held up by four Norman arches. In addition to two finely wrought Norman doorways, there are traces of wall-paintings on the arches and a triangular medieval nave window flanked by the stone faces of a man and a woman. The Lady Chapel has evocative stained-glass commemorations of the war dead, in the form of St Michael for the Royal Air Force and St Nicholas for the Royal Navy, together with three children in a tub.

The church also contains one of only four black marble Tournai fonts in the county and one of only ten still in existence, dating from around 1135 and exuberantly sculpted to portray the story of Adam and Eve and their expulsion from the Garden of Eden.

At **Warnford**, the Church of Our Lady, to the south of the village, was founded by St Wilfrid of York, the apostle to the Jutes of this area, who remained defiantly pagan well after the conversion of the West Saxons. The present church is evidently Norman in

Corhampton Church

Corhampton has a small early 11th-century Saxon church that is almost completely original and is one of the most important Saxon churches in southern England. The church looks as if it was built on an artificial mound and so may stand on the site of a pre-Christian temple. Its 12th-century wall-paintings in the chancel depict the life of St Swithun.

The church, comprising a nave and chancel, was constructed in about 1020 from local flints, locally available and inexpensive, which were then plastered over. The walls are very thin, only 2.5 feet (or 76cm) thick, strengthened by stone quoins shipped up the Meon from the Isle of Wight. The church survived substantially unaltered, except for the porch and some Norman and Early English details, together with a couple of buttresses and a vestry/boiler room, both added in the 19th century. The original east end, with a large round window, collapsed in 1842 when road widening weakened the foundations. In the churchyard, a Roman sarcophagus is being used for horticultural purposes.

character. Its rebuilt flint church holds the graves of the parents of Richard Cobden, the 19th-century exponent of social causes and Free Trade, and Thomas Lord, the founder and early proprietor of the London cricket ground that bears his name, who died in 1832. The village is a good centre for walks in the hills nearby and for access to the South Downs Way.

origin, with its large tower and carefully sculpted font, and it has interesting medieval and Jacobean features. The partial ruins of the 13th-century St John's or King John's House are nearby.

The Beacon Hill National Nature Reserve and SSSI are to the west of the parish, comprising a chalk hill that rises to 660 feet (201m) and several steep-sided valleys. The Monarch's Way long-distance footpath is within easy reach, as is the South Downs Way and access to the east to **Old Winchester Hill**, topped by a distinctive Iron Age fort and affording great views. The George and Falcon public house is a recom-mended place to stop for refreshment.

Soberton has another Meon church that has somehow gained a Roman coffin. The church is largely Early English, with a Perpendicular tower and many interesting features, notably its wall-paintings of saints and three 13th-century heads built into a wall.

Wickham is a market town (Leland called it a 'pretty townlet') neatly laid out around a large, attractive square, which had its origins as the fording place of the River Meon on the Roman road between *Noviomagus Regnorum* (Chichester) and *Venta Belgarum* (Winchester). The village of Wickham was

The Birthplace of Cricket

Hambledon is most famous for claims that it was the 'birthplace of cricket', although clubs in Kent and London certainly existed before local gentry formed the 'Hambledon Club' in the early 18th century, not least for the opportunities that cricket offered for betting. What is certain is that, by 1750, a local parish team, known then as 'Squire Land's Club', was attracting press and public attention and played a series of three matches against Dartford in 1756. Very quickly, Hambledon became the pre-eminent cricket club in England and in June 1777 defeated an All-England side at Sevenoaks in Kent by an innings and 168 runs.

The Hambledon Club declined in the 1780s when the focus for cricket moved from the counties of Kent, Hampshire and Sussex to London, where the Marylebone Cricket Club was established at Lord's in 1787. At this point, a major revision of the laws of the game was adopted, based on the improvements in the game that had been introduced and developed at Hambledon. On that basis, Hambledon should perhaps be known as the 'cradle' rather than the 'birthplace' of cricket!

Hambledon's original ground was at Broadhalfpenny Down, which is now the home of the Broadhalfpenny Brigands Cricket Club and where there is a monument. It shows the curved bat and two-stump wicket used in the early days. Opposite is the very convivial, but substantially restored 17th-century Bat and Ball public house, which used to be the original clubhouse and at which Hambledon's most famous captain, Richard Nyren, was landlord.

Wickham

first mentioned in history in 826. The Domesday Book noted that it had a population of about 120 in 1086 and two watermills on the river.

The town had a station on the Meon Valley Railway, planned in Victorian times as a direct route from London to the Isle of Wight, until the line closed in 1955. The track bed is now a most enjoyable cycle and walking route along the valley of the Meon, which can be accessed from the former station yard.

Its church, standing on its mound and outside the town, is certainly worth a visit. It has a fine Norman doorway and capitals sculpted with the Sagittarius badge of King Stephen, together with an exceptional Jacobean monument to Sir Willam Uvedale, scion of an ancient and substantial local family.

One of Nelson's captains from Trafalgar, Sir Richard Grindall of *HMS Prince*, is buried in the churchyard.

By the old railway bridge and opposite the church is Chesapeake Mill, constructed with timbers from the American frigate *Chesapeake,* which was captured off Boston by *HMS Shannon* in 1813.

A short diversion brings the visitor to **Hambledon**, an apparently Georgian village set in a shallow valley and contained within low wooded hills. The village itself is well worth an exploration on foot to reveal the hidden richness of its architectural heritage and a village whose antiquity of settlement is revealed by the significant Bronze and Iron Age evidence nearby and the remains of a substantial Roman villa to the south. It held a market under licence from the Bishops of Winchester in the Middle Ages and the original centre of the village was in the High Street, although East and West Street now shape its alignment.

With the village growing prosperous on agricultural produce, over 50 houses in Hambledon can be dated to the 17th century, although their origins have been obscured by brick facades of the 18th century and the presence of other buildings of the same period. Tower House in the High Street is a timber-framed structure that was been 'improved' in this way and Manor Farm in West Street is actually a 13th-century flint and stone manor house, with a 16th-century north wing and a Victorian west front. The 13th-century church of St Peter and St Paul, with traces of Saxon work, has a 15th-century porch and an 18th-century tower.

Places to Visit

Birdworld

Holt Pound, Nr Farnham, GU10 4LD
☎ 01420 22140
www.birdworld.co.uk
Open all year except 25 & 26 Dec.
Some restricted opening Nov to Feb.

Blue Reef Aquarium

Clarence Esplanade, Southsea,
PO5 3PB
☎ 023 9287 5222
www.bluereefaquarium.co.uk
Open daily (except Christmas Day)
from 10am.

Bursledon Windmill

Windmill Lane, Bursledon, SO31 8BG
☎ 0845 6035635
www.hants.gov.uk/museum/windmill
Open Sun and Bank Holiday Mon from
10am–4pm.

Bursledon Brickworks Industrial Museum

Coal Park Lane, Swanwick, SO31 7GW
☎ 01489 576248
www.bursledonbrickworks.co.uk
Regular Sun open days.

Butser Ancient Farm

Chalton Lane, Chalton, PO8 0BG
☎ 023 9259 8838
www.butser.org.uk
Open Easter to Sept from Mon–Fri only
unless there is a special event.

Charles Dickens Birthplace Museum

393 Old Commercial Road, Portsmouth,
PO1 4QL
☎ 023 9282 7261
www.charlesdickensbirthplace.co.uk
Open May to Sept 10.00am–5.30pm.
Closed from Oct to Apr inclusive,
except for Charles Dickens's Birthday, 7
Feb, 10.00am–5.00pm.

City Museum

3 Museum Rd, Portsmouth, PO1 2LE
☎ 023 92827261
www.portsmouthmuseums.co.uk
Open daily except 24–26 Dec. Apr to
Sept 10.00am–5.30pm. Oct to Mar
10.00am–5.00pm. Admission free

D Day Museum

Clarence Esplanade, Southsea,
PO5 3NT
☎ 023 9282 7261
www.ddaymuseum.co.uk
Open daily except 24–26 Dec. Apr to
Sept 10am–5.30pm (5pm Oct to Mar).

Domus Dei - Royal Garrison Church

Grand Parade, Old Portsmouth,
PO1 2NJ
☎ 023 9237 8291
www.english-heritage.org.uk
Open from Apr to Sept on Mon,
Tues, Thurs & Sat from 11am–4pm.
Admission free.

Explosion! The Museum of Naval Firepower

Priddy's Hard, Gosport, PO12 4LE
☎ 023 9250 5600
www.explosion.org.uk
Open 10am–4pm on Sat & Sun.

Fort Brockhurst

Gunner's Way, Elson, Gosport,
PO12 4DS
☎ 02392 581059
www.english-heritage.org.uk
Open on the 2nd Sat of every month
from Apr to Sep 11am–3pm.

Places to Visit

Funland Amusement Park

1 Seafront, Hayling Island, PO11 OAG
☎ 023 9246 2820
www.funland.info
Open daily in Jul, Aug & Easter School
Hol. Feb to May & Oct to Dec weekends
only. Open Wed–Sun in Jun. Closed
Jan. No admission charge but 'pay as
you ride'.

Gilbert White's House & the Oates Museum

The Wakes, Selborne, GU34 3JH
☎ 01420 511275
www.gilbertwhiteshouse.org.uk
Open daily Jun to Aug, Tue–Sun Sept to
May 11am–5pm. Closed Christmas week.

Hollycombe Steam Collection

Iron Hill, Liphook, Hants, GU30 7LP
☎ 01428 724900
www.hollycombe.co.uk
Open on Sun & some Sat Apr to Oct.
Some weekdays in Aug.

Natural History Museum

Cumberland House, Eastern Parade,
Southsea, PO4
☎ 023 9282 7261
www.portsmouthnaturalhistory.co.uk
Open daily except 24–26 Dec. Apr to
Oct 10am–5.30pm Nov to Mar 10am–
5.00pm. Admission free.

Portchester Castle

Castle St, Portchester, PO16 9QW
☎ 023 9237 8291
www.english-heritage.org.uk
Open every day except 25 & 26 Dec and
1 Jan from 10am–6pm (4pm in winter).

Portsmouth Historic Dockyard

Victory Gate, Portsmouth, PO1 3LJ
☎ 023 9272 8060
www.historicdockyard.co.uk
Open daily except 24–26 Dec from
10am–5pm.

HMS Victory
www.hms-victory.com

Royal Naval Museum
www.royalnavalmuseum.org

HMS Warrior 1860
www.hmswarrior.org

Mary Rose Museum & Ship Hall
www.maryrose.org

Action Stations
www.actionstations.org

Royal Marines Museum

Eastney Esplanade, Southsea, PO4 9PX
☎ 023 9281 9385
www.royalmarinesmuseum.co.uk
Open every day except 25 & 26 Dec
from 10am–5pm.

Royal Armouries Museum at Fort Nelson

Portsdown Hill Road, PO17 6AN
☎ 01329 233 734
www.royalarmouries.org
Open every day except 24–26 Dec. Apr
to Oct from 10am–5pm (opens at 11am
on Wed) & Nov to Mar from 10.30am–
4pm (opens at 11.30am on Wed).

Royal Navy Submarine Museum

Haslar Jetty Road, Gosport, PO12 2AS
☎ 023 9252 9217
www.rnsubmus.co.uk
Open every day except 24 Dec–2 Jan
from 10am – 5.30pm (4.30pm in winter).

Southsea Castle

Clarence Parade, Southsea, PO5 3PA
☎ 023 9282 7261
www.southseacastle.co.uk
Open Daily Apr to Sept 10am–5.30pm.

Spitbank Fort

The Solent, off Portsmouth
☎ 01329 242077
www.spitbankfort.co.uk
Opening times vary, check on website.

Spinnaker Tower

Gunwharf Quays, Portsmouth, PO1 3TT
☎ 023 9285 7520
www.spinnakertower.co.uk
Open daily from 10am (except
Christmas Day).

Stansted Park

Nr Rowlands Castle, PO9 6DX
☎ 023 9241 2265
For details see www.stanstedpark.co.uk
Just across the Hampshire border.

Titchfield Abbey

North of A27, Titchfield, PO15 5RA
☎ 023 92 378291
www.english-heritage.org.uk
Open daily Apr to Sep 10am–5pm; Oct
to Mar 10am–4pm; closed 24–26 Dec
and 1 Jan. Admission free.

Westbury Manor Museum

West St, Fareham, PO16 0JJ
☎ 0845 6035635
www.hants.gov.uk/museum/westbury-
manor-museum
Open all year Mon–Fri 10am–5pm &
Sat 10am–4pm. Closed Christmas.
Admission free

The National Gardens Scheme

Opening dates and times of gardens in
and around
Portsmouth and East Hampshire are
available on
the website: www.ngs.org,uk

COUNTRY PARKS

Alice Holt Forest

Bucks Horn Oak, Nr Farnham, GU10 4LS
☎ 01420 23666
www.forestry.gov.uk/aliceholt
On the Hampshire/Surrey border a few
miles south of Farnham on the A325.
Open all year 8am–5pm (Oct to Feb),
7pm (Mar, April & Sept), 9pm (May to
Aug). Car parking charges apply.

Manor Farm Country Park

Pylands Lane, Bursledon, SO31 1BH
☎ 01489 787055
www.hants.gov.uk/manorfarm
The Country Park is open daily.
Admission free. Manor Farm is open
daily April to Oct and on Sun Nov to
March from 10am–5pm.

Queen Elizabeth Country Park

Gravel Hill, Horndean, PO8 0QE.
☎ 023 9259 5040
www.hants.gov.uk/qecp
Open daily. Visitor Centre, Shop & Café
open Mar to Oct 10am–5.30pm; Nov to
22 Dec 10am–4.30pm. Admission free.
Parking charges apply.

Staunton Country Park

Middle Park Way, Havant, PO9 5HB
☎ 023 9245 3405
www.hants.gov.uk/hampshire-
countryside/staunton
Open daily 10am–5pm (4pm in winter).

Titchfield Haven National Nature Reserve

Cliff Road Hill Head PO14 3JT
☎ 01329 662145
www.hants.gov.uk/hampshire-
countryside/titchfield
Open Wed–Sun and Bank Holidays
from 9.30am–5pm (4pm in winter).
Closed 25 & 26 Dec. Admission charge
to reserve.

5. The New Forest

With a landscape, culture and physical character unlike any other in Hampshire, the New Forest comprises 145 very accessible square miles (375 sq km) and is largely unenclosed and uncultivated.

It lies in the south-west corner of Hampshire, stretching from east of the Avon Valley to Southampton Water and from the Solent coast to the edge of the Wiltshire Downs. Probably settled by the Jutes in the years after Roman influence and power declined and taken over by the West Saxon kings, it was enclosed and protected by Forest Law under the Normans and maintained as a royal hunting leisure park for much of the medieval period. Interestingly, the soils of the area were (and still are) largely infertile and unsuitable for large-scale cultivation of the land. This has been the main reason why it was not cleared and why it was actually a clever move by the Normans to use it for recreation. It is more or less contained within the *New Forest National Park*, which was created in 2005 and is the newest and smallest National Park in England.

The highest point in the New Forest is **Piper's Wait** (410ft/125m), just west of Bramshaw, and the area is drained to the south by the rivers Lymington and Beaulieu. The Forest is famous for the wide range of native animal species, its indigenous and eponymous ponies in particular, which wander freely, and all

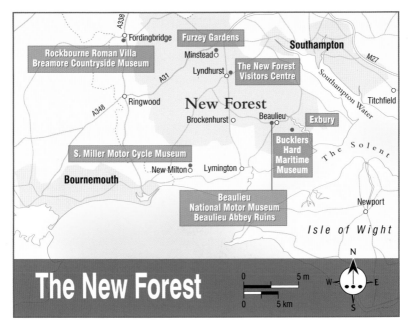

Fordingbridge

Furzey Gardens

Minstead

Southampton

**Rockbourne Roman Villa
Breamore Countryside Museum**

Lyndhurst

**The New Forest
Visitors Centre**

M27

Southampton Water

Titchfield

Ringwood

New Forest

Brockenhurst

Beaulieu

Exbury

The Solent

S. Miller Motor Cycle Museum

**Bucklers
Hard
Maritime
Museum**

New Milton

Lymington

Bournemouth

Newport

**Beaulieu
National Motor Museum
Beaulieu Abbey Ruins**

Isle of Wight

The New Forest

0   5 m

0   5 km

N

W   E

S

the Forest roads have speed limit of no more than 40mph. Drivers are frequently warned about the likelihood of animals close to the edge of the road, and about 100 animals – and some humans – are either killed or injured as a result of collisions with cars each year. The Forest provides, of course, excellent opportunities for walking, riding and cycling, at all levels of fitness and inclination.

The 'capital' of the New Forest is

The New Forest

Lyndhurst, a popular tourist destination which, largely because of the one-way road system, is generally a traffic hot-spot in the summer months. Nevertheless, it is popular with visitors and a good starting point for an introduction to the unique culture of the Forest and for expeditions into its interior. The museum, now part of the New Forest Centre, tells the story of this distinctive landscape and habitat with exhibitions demonstrating its geology and history through the centuries right up to modern times. At the top of the main street is the Gothic-style church of St Michael's and All Angels, the last resting place of Alice Hargreaves, the inspiration for Lewis Carroll's 'Alice in Wonderland'. She lived in Lyndhurst most of her life and there is a memorial in the baptistry to her two sons, who died within a week of each other in the

The Court of Verderers and Traditions of the New Forest

This ancient governing body consists of ten members or *verderers*, half appointed, half elected, who are responsible for regulating the activities of those Forest animals which belong to the commoners. They are assisted by full-time keepers or *agisters* who have responsibility for a specific area of the Forest and who register and monitor the animals, all bearing the owner's or *commoner's* brand mark. Today, about 450 commoners make use of these ancient rights but 'commoning' does not provide a full-time living and so many commoners support themselves through other means. An additional problem, in the 21st century, is that many properties with common rights have been bought as retirement or second homes and the new owners are not continuing the 'commoning' tradition. The New Forest Ponies, together with the cattle and deer, give this beautiful area its distinctive character and are vital for the preservation and balance of landscape. Without them, the Forest would soon become overgrown and many species would be unsustainable, so it is vital that, with the support of the National Park and other authorities, this ancient forest tradition continues.

There are six ancient rights of common attached to particular lands and properties in the New Forest. Some are rarely or no longer invoked, but the most important are:

• *The common of mast* – pigs can be turned out in autumn to devour the acorns, to reduce the poison risk to ponies and cattle.

• *The common of turbary* - a commoner can cut peat turfs for his or her personal use.

• *Estovers* – the free supply of a stipulated amount of firewood to certain properties.

• *The common of pasture* – commoners are entitled to let their cattle, ponies, donkeys and mules roam freely in the Open Forest.

First World War. There is also an arresting fresco which was painted by Lord Frederick Leighton in 1860, as well as stained-glass windows designed by the Pre-Raphaelite artists Burne-Jones, Rossetti and William Morris. Nearby, The Queen's House is the headquarters of the Forestry Commission, the body that looks after the forest plantations, roads and paths, and ensures that invasive, aggressive plants, such as rhododendrons and gorse, do not threaten other species. Lyndhurst is also where the Courtroom of the Verderers has existed since 1388 to deal with disputes and issues affecting Forest law and local custom. On the eastern side of Lyndhurst, close to the town centre is Bolton's Bench. With its open grassy lawns and cricket pitch it is a good spot to relax or have a picnic if the weather is fine.

Two miles (3km) to the south of Lyndhurst is New Park, the location of the **New Forest and Hampshire County Show** which takes place at the end of July each year. This three-day show attracts thousands of visitors from miles around and, as one of the UK's top agricultural shows, it celebrates and perpetuates the countryside and traditions of the New Forest.

Brockenhurst lies halfway between Lymington and Lyndhurst on the main London to Weymouth railway line. One of the first things to be seen on arrival is the Balmer Lawn Hotel. In the New Forest the word 'lawn' means an area of closely cropped grassland which provides the best animal grazing. The 200-acre (80ha) Balmer Lawn was once the site of a racetrack where New Forest ponies raced! This area is popular with campers and caravanners who are well provided for with excellent camping and caravanning sites discreetly located at a respectable distance from the village. This means that Brockenhurst retains a sleepy, traditional feel.

To the south of the railway line, set apart from the main village and situated on top of a hill, is the church of St Nicholas. This gem is supposedly the oldest church in the Forest and there is evidence of Saxon stonework in the south door. Outside the church is an ancient yew tree which has been carbon dated and is over 1,000 years old, and in the churchyard is the grave of a well-known local character called Brusher Mills who died in 1905 and 'for a number of years followed the occupation of snake-catcher in the New Forest'. He made a living by supplying London Zoo with adders for snake-eating animals and one of the local pubs he used to frequent is now called The Snakecatcher in his memory! The Anzac War Cemetery is also here with the graves of nearly 100 New Zealanders who died as a result of injuries sustained during the First World War. The No.1 New Zealand General Hospital was based at Brockenhurst from 1916 to 1919.

On the outskirts of Brockenhurst is the **Rhinefield Ornamental Drive**, which runs past the Rhinefield House Hotel and continues northwards to the A35 Lyndhurst to Christchurch Road. The best time of year to see the drive in all its splendour is in May and June, when the rhododendron bushes are full of colour. There are also giant redwoods and two of the tallest trees in the New Forest, which were planted in the mid 19th century.

On the way to Lymington is **Boldre**, which has wonderful views of the New Forest and the Isle of Wight. St John the Baptist's Church has a memorial to the 1,418 seamen who were lost in May 1941 when *HMS Hood* was sunk by the German battleship Bismarck (there were only three survivors). **Spinners**, a garden which is open from April to September, has a dazzling display of magnolias, azaleas, hydrangeas and rhododendrons on wooded slopes leading down to the Lymington River.

Lymington dates back at least to the 12th century and is a charming New Forest town with an unhurried, steady atmosphere. Its port, which in the past was a centre for boatbuilding, sustains the ferry traffic to Yarmouth in the Isle of Wight and is home to a great many yachts and leisure craft. Its broad High Street is lined with a variety of mainly 18th-century houses and local retailers and in past centuries it was notorious for its smuggling history. There are supposed to be tunnels leading from the town quay to the old inns under the High Street. **Quay Hill** has a particularly tempting selection of small quality shops, while at the top of the High Street, St Thomas's Church dates back

A beautiful view of the New Forest

to 1250. The river is lined with all sorts of craft and businesses which live off the yachting industry, and the sights, sounds and smells of the sea are never very far away. Each Saturday, a market is held in the High Street, the origins of which probably date back to the 13th century. The **St Barbe Museum** explores the town's unique history and that of the Solent shore with accounts of smugglers, salterns and boatbuilders.

The Solent Way, the coastal path at this point follows the right bank of the Lymington River and heads south-west parallel to the coast through an area of outstanding beauty: the **Lymington to Keyhaven Nature Reserve**. At **Keyhaven**, a small, tucked-away village, one can look across the water to the impressively sited **Hurst Castle**, which was built at the end of a very narrow 1½ mile (2km) long shingle spit. Access can be gained either by walking along the Hurst Beach spit or, conditions permitting, on the small ferry which leaves from Keyhaven on a regular basis. Either way, the journey is well worth the effort. Dominating the western approach to the Solent, Hurst Castle is just ¾ mile (1km) from the Isle of Wight and was built in 1544, again as part of Henry VIII's strategic chain of artillery fortresses. After the Civil War, in 1648, it was a prison

for Charles I when he was en route from Carisbrooke Castle in the Isle of Wight to his trial and subsequent execution in London. The excellent position of Hurst Castle ensured that further fortification and modernisation took place in the 19th century and it was manned until the end of the Second World War.

From Keyhaven, the road takes you through the traditional and unspoilt village of **Milford on Sea**. The 'on Sea' part of its name was added at the end of the 19th century because a local landowner planned in vain to make Milford a premier seaside resort. Originally a Saxon settlement, which belonged to Christchurch Priory (now in Dorset) in the Middle Ages, much of Milford's wealth in the past was derived from agriculture and the sea (sea salt and smuggling). The church of All Saints was used as a smugglers' lookout post and a store for contraband goods.

Both Milford on Sea and nearby **New Milton** are just outside the Forest boundaries, close to the Dorset border. New Milton is another settlement with Saxon origins but developed as a thriving Victorian community with its own railway station, on the main London to Weymouth line. Barton on Sea, now part of New Milton, can be a good place to look for fossils although it is not always possible to access the cliffs

Horses grazing in the New Forest

Fallow Deer

as they are subject to coastal erosion and it is advisable to take care and heed warning notices. **The Sammy Miller Motor Cycle Museum** in New Milton has one of the finest collections in Europe, consisting of over 400 fully restored motorcycles spanning seven decades, and is dedicated to the golden age of British motorcycling. Also in New Milton is one of Hampshire's most expensive hotels, the five-star Chewton Glen which has a famous literary link. Captain Frederick Marryat stayed here when the house belonged to his brother in the 1840s and found inspiration for his novel, *The Children of the New Forest*. Much of the action of this book, a tale of the English Civil War, was set in and around the parish of **Sway** which lies to the east. The origins of the name Sway come from *Svieia*, which means 'noisy water' and no doubt refers to the nearby Avon. The village is sited at the heart of the New Forest and has its own station on the main Waterloo to Weymouth line. One of the first things that any visitor sees is a 218ft (66m) high tower known as Peterson's Tower. This Victorian folly was built between 1879 and 1885 by an eccentric Victorian judge, Andrew Peterson, who had spent his working life in India. He was fascinated by the use of unreinforced concrete in building and insisted that Sir Christopher Wren had advised him on his project through a spiritualist medium! It is supposedly

the oldest concrete building in the UK and the second tallest folly in the world. Intended as a mausoleum for Judge Peterson, it was damaged during the 1987 hurricane, but restored with the help of English Heritage. Formerly a Bed and Breakfast establishment, these days it is a private family home and a communication mast – *sic transit gloria mundi*!

Opposite Lymington, on the left bank of the river is the Wightlink car ferry terminal which takes passengers and their vehicles to and from Yarmouth on the Isle of Wight. On this side of the river, the road heads north-east through open heathland and via the brown tourist signs to the picturesque port of **Bucklers Hard** on the Beaulieu River with its Maritime Museum and planned model village around which, in the 18th century, the 2nd Duke of Montagu made grand plans to create Montagu Town. The intention was to import sugar from

St Barbe Museum, Lymington

Sammy Miller Motorcycle Museum

plantations in the West Indies, but the French beat him to it; the duke lost a fortune and his plans for a major port had to be scaled down. Buckler's Hard retained its original name and, with so many oak trees in its vicinity, became a major centre for building wooden warships. Four of these ships fought at the Battle of Trafalgar, but the business collapsed at the end of the Napoleonic Wars in 1815 after failing to deliver four ships to the Admiralty on time. The Georgian village remains part of the Beaulieu estate. The **Maritime Museum** documents the history of Bucklers Hard and the old Master Shipbuilder's House, which once belonged to Henry Adams, is now a hotel overlooking the river.

A little further up the river, **Beaulieu**, one of the New Forest's major attractions, is extremely popular with visitors and has something for all age groups. At the beginning of the 13th century, King John founded a Cistercian abbey named *Bellus Locus* in the heart of the forest. Translated into Norman French, it was known as Beaulieu, a '*fair place*'. The abbey church was modelled on the French monastery of Clairvaux and was dedicated in 1246. At the Dissolution, the abbey and manor were purchased by Thomas Wriothesley, later 1st Earl of Southampton, and much of the abbey church was demolished. Many of the stones from the abbey were recycled and used in the new fortifications built to protect the south coast from the French at Hurst, Calshot and Cowes. Today, apart from the clearly marked outline of the abbey church, only a few buildings remain from the Middle Ages, including the cloisters, the former refectory, which is now Beaulieu Abbey Church, and part of the former monastery gatehouse and inner hall which were incorporated into a manor house (Palace House).

In the 18th century, Palace House and the Beaulieu estate passed into the family of the Dukes of Buccleuch. The 5th Duke gave it to his second son, the 1st Baron Montagu of Beaulieu, as a wedding present, and extensive alterations were carried out in the 1870s. The current owner, Lord Montagu, inherited the estate from his father in 1929, when he was three years old, and, in 1952, he opened Beaulieu to the public. He installed five cars in the front hall of the house as a tribute to his father's passion for motoring and the **National Motor Museum** was born. These days, the purpose-built museum houses more than 250 vehicles from every motoring generation and caters for a variety of tastes and age groups. For younger visitors, there is a chance to drive mini motorised vehicles or go-karts. For anyone who does not want to walk through the gardens to the abbey ruins or Palace House, there is a convenient

The Spirit of Ecstasy

This famous car logo and mascot, designed by Charles Sykes, has been associated with the Rolls-Royce marquee since 1911. The idea for the original design, 'the Whisper', came from the 2nd Lord Montagu of Beaulieu, who commissioned a mascot for the radiator of his Rolls Royce Silver Ghost.

The model was Eleanor Thornton, who was Lord Montagu's secretary and reputedly his mistress. Sadly, she lost her life only a few years later, when, on 30 December 1915, the *SS Persia*, en route for India, was torpedoed off Crete. Lord Montagu was also on board, but survived.

monorail. Throughout the year, Beaulieu also hosts regular, well-attended special events, such as auto and boat jumbles.

From Beaulieu, the road to Lyndhurst goes past Beaulieu Road Station, where pony sales are held six times per year. There is an option to head towards Southampton by crossing the Beaulieu River and driving past the old entrance to Beaulieu Abbey. A short drive leads to the Rothschilds' **Exbury Gardens** at the eastern mouth of the Beaulieu River, with its particularly impressive array of shrubs and flowers. The estate was bought just after the First World War by Lionel Nathan de Rothschild, who described himself as 'a banker by hobby, a gardener by profession'. After two decades and one million plantings, he had created a magnificent 200-acre (80ha) garden. During the Second World War, Exbury was requisitioned by the Royal Navy and commissioned as *HMS Mastodon*, which was the main setting for Nevil Shute's novel, *Requiem for a Wren*. In 1955, Lionel's son, Edmund, who shared his father's lifelong passion, opened the gardens to the public. 'Mr Eddy', as he was affectionately known, was an internationally renowned figure in horticulture, especially for his cultivation of rhododendrons and azaleas. Exbury reflects this commitment and expertise and those who love visiting gardens will be not be disappointed by the marvellous seasonal displays, which also feature camellias and magnolias.

Just beyond the village of Exbury is **Lepe Coastal Country Park**, with a mile-long (1.5km) beach (watch out for rip tides) and stunning views across the Solent to the Isle of Wight. In fine weather, this is just the place for the family, with a play area and barbecues for hire.

On returning through Exbury and rejoining the B3054, one cannot avoid the 3,200-acre (1,300ha) Fawley Oil Refinery and the 650ft (200m) Fawley power station chimney, which is visible from a considerable distance in all directions. Beyond Fawley is **Calshot Castle**, on the western edge of Southampton Water, another of Henry VIII's chain of coastal defences. The stones for this cleverly placed fortification came from Beaulieu Abbey and most probably from Netley Abbey on the opposite side of Southampton Water. These days it is part of the **Calshot Activities Centre**, one of the largest outdoor adventure centres in Britain. Owned by Hampshire County Council, it boasts a 12,000 square foot (1,200 sq m) climbing facility, a dry ski slope and an indoor velodrome. Residential and non-residential courses are available throughout the year.

Hythe overlooks Southampton Water and the **Hythe Ferry** takes foot passengers to and from Southampton Town Quay in just twelve minutes. To embark on the ferry, passengers travel along a Victorian pier on a narrow-gauge electric train, claimed to be the world's oldest pier train. Much restoration work has been carried out on the pier which was severed by a drunken dredger skipper in 2003. When the large cruise ships, such as the *Queen Mary 2* and the *Queen Victoria*, are alongside in Southampton, the Hythe Ferry affords passengers a splendid view of the cruise liners, as it passes close by the Cunard berth.

Also on the edge of Southampton Water, but on the outskirts of the New Forest, **Eling Tide Mill** is one of the last of its kind in the world. The oldest reference to a mill on the site is in the Domesday Survey of 1086 although it is thought that there has been a tidal milling facility here since Roman times. Restored in the late 1970s, it is a unique example of Hampshire's industrial heritage, which periodically harnesses the power of the tide to grind wheat into the flour sold in the shop.

At **Ashurst** there are signs for **Longdown Activity Farm**, an enjoyable attraction which appeals to children with opportunities for hands-on activities and daily feeding schedules. Bottle-feeding kid goats and calves, duck feeding and small animal handling are just some of the things to do and there are several play areas both indoors and outdoors in which children can run around. Further on is the **New Forest Otter and Wildlife Park** where there are, amongst other animals, pine martens, polecats, minks, stoats, badgers, wallabies, wild boar and deer. The park is involved in conservation work and cares for orphaned otters, with facilities to care for injured or orphaned wild animals.

Nearby **Cadnam** is a hamlet on the eastern edge of the forest, immediately adjacent to a large roundabout leading to junction 1 of the M27 motorway and the A31. From the roundabout there are brown tourist signs directing visitors to the **Rufus Stone**, which is on the north side of the A31. The stone marks the spot where King William II (Rufus) was killed by an arrow in 1100 while out hunting in the Forest. Whether his death was the result of an accident or a calculated act of political assassination is not known for certain, but his hunting companions, including Sir Walter Tyrell (the alleged perpetrator), dispersed in haste and William's younger brother, Henry, sped off suspiciously quickly to secure the Treasury at Winchester and seize the throne. The king's body was unceremoniously taken to Winchester on a forester's cart and buried in the cathedral.

This part of the forest is criss-crossed with excellent footpaths and bridleways and several small villages, most of them with popular, and sometimes picturesque, pubs. **Brook**, with its thatched cottages, has the oldest golf club in Hampshire, while **Fritham** village and **Eyeworth Pond** offer good opportunities for deer spotting. **Bramshaw** was mentioned in the Domesday Survey and archaeological digs have revealed evidence of Stone Age implements and Roman pottery. **Bramshaw Commons** are owned by the National Trust, but the animals are managed by the Court of Verderers. And just to the west of Bramshaw

Palace House Beaulieu

Exbury Gardens

is the highest point of the New Forest at Piper's Wait (410ft/125m), another popular starting point for walks.

Minstead, just to the south of the A31, is a small village with a cluster of houses and the perennially popular Trusty Servant Inn overlooking the village green. The unusual church of All Saints, with its distinctive Georgian brick tower, is a jumble of architectural styles which range from the 12th to the 18th centuries. It has a three-decker pulpit and two extraordinary family pews; one with its own fireplace! In the churchyard is the grave of Sir Arthur Conan Doyle, author of the Sherlock Holmes stories. Minstead is also home to **Furzey Gardens**, originally designed and planted in 1922. With eight acres (3ha) of flowering trees and shrubs and an extensive collection of azaleas and rhododendrons, it has viewpoints across the New Forest to the Isle of Wight. The garden is a delight all year round and during the summer visits to the restored 16th-century thatched New Forest cottage and the Craft Gallery are a justifiable use of time.

From Minstead, it is possible to rejoin the A31 and turn off at Stoney Cross towards the small hamlet of **Emery Down** with the popular New Forest Inn. Next to the pub is a minor forest road leading to several car parks, ideal for walkers and very near to the **New Forest Reptile Centre** at Holidays Hill Enclosure (also accessible by car from the A35). This small conservation centre, for which there is no entry charge, has examples of all Britain's reptiles in one place: adders, grass snakes, smooth snakes, lizards, frogs and toads are in separate, open-air, netted pens. Further along the road is the **Bolderwood Deer Sanctuary** where viewing platforms overlook a fenced area in which a number of fallow deer are kept. Deer sightings are not necessarily guaranteed, but as the herd is fed each afternoon at 2pm (April to September) by the local New Forest keeper, the deer are more than happy to remain in the main meadow.

On the same road, not far from the A31 is the simple **Canadian Memorial** to the 3rd Canadian Division, recalling those troops who were based in the New Forest before they travelled across the Channel to Normandy in June 1944. From here, the narrow road leads to **Bolderwood Arboretum Ornamental Drive**. This scenic drive through

Grishkin at the New Forest Otter and Wildlife Park

ancient and ornamental woodlands is very busy during the summer months, but note should be made in passing of the Knightwood Oak Tree, the largest and probably oldest (about 400 years) oak tree in the New Forest. The drive ends at the A35 about two miles (3km) west of Lyndhurst and opposite the entrance to Rhinefield Ornamental Drive (see under Brockenhurst).

Nestled between the A31 and the A35, just to the east of Ringwood, is the traditional New Forest village of **Burley**, popular with visitors not least because of its quaint tearooms and gift shops, many of which have a witchcraft theme. After the 1735 Witchcraft Act was repealed in 1951, Sybil Leek, who ran an antiques shop in Burley, declared herself a white witch. This aroused much interest in the media and tourists flocked to the village. Eventually Sybil Leek moved to the United States where she died in 1982 and her former shop changed its name to 'A Coven of Witches'! During the summer, there are numerous antique and craft fairs as well as a monthly Sunday food market. Burley has several pubs and hotels which make it a popular base from which to explore the Forest, including the chance to take a tractor and trailer ride to see the deer in Burley Park. Close to the post office there is the New Forest Cider Shop and Gallery.

The traffic on the A31 speeds past **Ringwood** as motorists head for Bournemouth, the Poole ferry and the West Country. This small market town is on the River Avon, which now marks the county boundary between Hampshire and Dorset. Dating back to the 11th century, 'Ringvede', as it was called, was granted its market charter in 1226 and, as well as having a good choice of independent shops, its market still

takes place every Wednesday. In 1685, the Duke of Monmouth was betrayed whilst hiding at nearby Horton after the Battle of Sedgemoor. He was taken to a house in West Street, now known as Monmouth House, and then to the Tower of London, where he was brought to trial and executed.

Close to the river on the south side of the town is the **Ringwood Brewery**, founded in 1978 on the site of an older brewery, which produces intriguingly named beers such as *Huffkin*, *Old Thumper* and *Boondoggle*. During the summer, there are usually brewery tours once a week for adults and children over 14 years but bookings should be made in advance. Also of interest and close by, at the aptly named Crow, is the **Liberty Owl, Raptor and Reptile Centre**, home to a large collection of birds of prey, snakes, lizards and tortoises and with daily displays which are subject to weather conditions.

Just across the county border in Ringwood Forest is the **Moors Valley Country Park** which has 20 miles (30km) of waymarked trails and a host of other activities. For more information see www.moors-valley.co.uk. Also close to Ringwood, but just in Dorset, is the **Avon Heath Country Park**, a very special heathland habitat and home to two internationally rare species of birds: the Dartford Warbler and the Nightjar (see www.dorsetforyou.com/avon-heath).

The **Avon Valley Path**, set up in 1992, is 34 miles (55km) long and follows the Hampshire and Wiltshire Avon from the mouth of the river at Christchurch through Ringwood and Fordingbridge north to Downton and Salisbury.

Blashford Lakes Nature Reserve,

north of Ringwood, along the Avon Valley, is a series of former gravel pits which are now a 490-acre (200ha) wildlife reserve visited by thousands of wildfowl every winter and managed by the Hampshire Wildlife Trust. The Nature Reserve is an excellent spot for birdwatching and there are various walking routes through the reserve as well as a site education centre.

Here, too, is the village of **Ellingham**, where Dame Alice Lisle's tomb can be found to the right of the south door of St Mary's Church. She was charged with harbouring fugitives from the Battle of Sedgemoor and was executed for treason in Winchester in 1685 on the orders of Judge Jeffreys. The local pub, formerly the village school, is now known as the Alice Lisle Inn.

As **Fordingbridge's** name suggests, the bridge with its seven graceful arches sits astride the Hampshire Avon, which rises about 3 miles (5km) east of Devizes in Wiltshire. The first known bridge was built in about 1286 and there are some attractive walks along the river banks. There is also a riverside park with views of the Great Bridge, near which there is a bronze statue of the painter, Augustus John, who moved to Fordingbridge in 1927 and lived at Studio North until his death in 1961. It is said that he often rode his horse bareback to the local pub, eccentrically patting the heads of all the children he passed, on the basis that he might have fathered them! The Fordingbridge museum, located in the old granary, houses an exhibition on this bohemian artist and records the social history of Fordingbridge through pictures and artefacts.

The Church of St Mary was listed in the Domesday Survey in the late 11th century, extended throughout the Middle Ages, but has changed very little since the 16th century, having escaped Victorian remodelling. A new stained-glass window was commissioned to commemorate the Millennium and two of the bells were recast and retuned at the Whitechapel Bell Foundry. In the churchyard, there is a monument to the Chubb family, whose firm is renowned for its safes and locks, as well as a memorial to John Alexander Seton, killed in the last recorded duel fought in England in 1845.

Branksome China has been in Fordingbridge since 1966, although the company, with its innovative designs, was founded in 1945 by Ernest Baggaley on the outskirts of Bournemouth. The shop sells fine porcelain tableware as well as a range of various animal studies that include New Forest ponies.

A few miles to the north-west of Fordingbridge is **Rockbourne Roman Villa**, which was discovered in 1942 by a farmer trying to retrieve his ferret from a rabbit hole. He found oyster shells and tiles and a local amateur archaeologist spent the next 30 years unearthing the largest known villa in the area, with a history spanning 350 years. These days the site is looked after by Hampshire County Council museums service. It is possible to walk around the remains of the villa and visit the museum that houses many of the fascinating site finds. Not far from the villa is a 100ft (30m) column erected in 1827 in memory of the famous Indian Army General Sir Eyre Coote and his nephew, also a general, who lived at West Park (burnt down in the 1940s). There are further monuments to the Coote family in Rockbourne's St Andrew's Church in the centre of this charming Hampshire village.

Breamore House

The **Martin Peninsula** borders Dorset and Wiltshire just to the west of Rockbourne. The naturalist and ornithologist, W.H. Hudson, described this area (originally in South Wiltshire) and the way of life in his book *A Shepherd's Life*, published in 1910. Off the beaten track, the most westerly Hampshire village of Martin is on the edge of Martin Down, a National Nature Reserve. One of the largest areas of chalk downland in England, it is dotted with many ancient monuments, burial mounds and earthworks.

Worth a Look

St Mary's Church at Breamore is one of the most important Saxon buildings in the county and dates from about 1000. It is an almost complete example of a Saxon Romanesque flint church and is exceptionally long (96ft 6in or 29.5m), consisting of a chancel and a nave without aisles and a square central tower, from which originally led a chapel or transept on each side. The northern transept has now disappeared, along with a nave extension to the west. The walls were built with flints with large quoins and pilaster strips of green sandstone and ironstone. Apart from the rebuilt 14th-century chancel and the south porch, the church is remarkably unaltered and it has a Saxon inscription over the south transept arch, meaning, 'Here the Word is manifested to you'.

Worth a Visit

Just off the main Fordingbridge to Salisbury road, travellers will catch a glimpse of a distinctive rose-red brick house at **Breamore** (pronounced Bremmer), which is set in a park surrounded by farmland and overlooks the Avon valley. Originally built in 1583 for the Dodington family, Breamore House has been in the Hulse family since 1748. Much of the house interior was rebuilt after a fire in 1856, but it is a charming family manor house with some fine paintings, tapestries and period furniture.

Those who feel like a stroll and a visit to something curious can follow the public footpath through the grounds of **Breamore House** to the ancient, possibly prehistoric Breamore Mizmaze, a scheduled monument, which is one of only eight remaining English turf labyrinths. It is thought that, in medieval times, penances took place here, with penitents going around the maze on their knees and saying prayers at appropriate points.

Breamore Countryside Museum has re-creations of the village buildings and workshops of a 17th-century village. There is also a collection of steam-powered farm machinery and an adventure playground for younger children.

Places to Visit

Beaulieu: National Motor Museum, Beaulieu Abbey Ruins & Palace House

Beaulieu, SO42 7ZN
☎ 01590 612345
www.beaulieu.co.uk
Open daily except Christmas Day from 10am–5pm (6pm Jun to Sept).

Bolderwood Deer Sanctuary

www.new-forest-national-park.com/
bolderwood-deer-sanctuary
The herd are fed daily by the local New Forest keeper, between Apr and Sept.

Branksome China

Shaftesbury St, Fordingbridge, SP6 1JF
☎ 01425 652010
www.branksomechina.co.uk
Open Mon–Sat from 10am–5pm.

Breamore House & Countryside Museum

Near Fordingbridge, SP6 2DF
☎ 01725 512468
www.breamorehouse.com
House: 2–5.30pm. Last guided tour 4pm.
Countryside Museum: 1–5.30pm.
Open Apr: Tue and Sun only and Easter weekend; May to Sept Tue, Wed, Thur, Sat, Sun and all Bank Holidays.

Bucklers Hard

Bucklers Hard, SO42 7XB.
Follow brown tourist signs
☎ 01590 616203
www.bucklershard.co..uk
Open every day except Christmas Day.
Optional extra 30 minute river cruise.

Calshot Castle

Calshot Spit, Fawley, SO45 1BR
☎ 023 8089 2077
www.calshot.com
Open Apr to Sept daily 10.30am–4.30pm.

Eling Tide Mill

The Tollbridge, Totton, SO40 9HF
☎ 023 80 869575
www.elingtidemill.wanadoo.co.uk
Open Wed–Sun 10am–4pm and Bank Holiday Mon (Closed Christmas and Boxing Day).

Go Ape

Moors Valley Country Park, Horton Rd, Ashley Heath, Ringwood, BH24 2ET
☎ 0845 643 9215
www.goape.co.uk

Hurst Castle

Keyhaven, SO41 0TR
☎ 01590 642344
www.hurstcastle.co.uk
Open daily from Apr to Sept 10.30am–5.30pm daily in Oct and weekends only Nov to Mar 10.30am–4pm.

Liberty's Owl, Raptor & Reptile Centre

Crow Lane, Ringwood, BH24 3EA
☎ 01425 476487
www.libertyscentre.co.uk
Open daily Mar to Oct 10am–5pm.
Weekends only Nov–Feb 10am–4pm.

Longdown Activity Farm

Ashurst, Near Lyndhurst, SO40 7EH
☎ 023 8029 3326
www.longdownfarm.co.uk
Open daily mid-Feb to Oct from 10am–5pm. Open weekends in Nov and Dec.

The New Forest Centre

Lyndhurst, SO43 7NY
☎ 023 8028 3444
www.newforestcentre.org.uk
Open daily 10am–5pm. Closed 24-26 Dec, 31 Jan & 1 Feb. Pay & Display Car Park.

New Forest Otter, Owl & Wildlife Park

Deerleap Lane, Longdown, SO40 4UH
☎ 023 8029 2408
www.ottersandowls.co.uk
Open daily from 10am. Closing times vary seasonally.

Places to Visit

New Forest Reptile Centre

Holidays Hill, Nr Lyndhurst - ordanance survey map No 1095 grid ref 269072. Car park charge.

Sammy Miller Motorcycle Museum

Bashley Cross Rd, New Milton, BH25 5SZ
☎ 01425 616644
www.sammymiller.co.uk
Open daily 10am–4.30pm.

St Barbe Museum & Art Gallery

New Street, Lymington, SO41 9BH
☎ 01590 676 969
www.stbarbe-museum.org.uk
Open Mon–Sat 10am–4pm.

Rockbourne Roman Villa

Near Fordingbridge, SP6 3PG
☎ 0845 603 5635
Open late Mar to Sept daily 10.30am–6pm.

GARDENS

Apple Court at Hordle

Hordle Lane, Hordle, Lymington, SO41 OHU
☎ 01590 642130
www.applecourt.com
A mile from the coast, this one acre walled garden specialises in day lilies, hostas, ferns and grasses.

Exbury Gardens

Exbury, SO45 1AZ.
☎ 023 8089 1203
www.exbury.co.uk
Open Mar to Nov daily from 10am–5pm. Santa Specials in Dec. Mr Eddy's Restaurant and Tearooms, Gift shop and Plant centre facilities may be used by all, not just visitors to the garden.

Furzey Gardens

School Lane, Minstead, SO43 7GL
☎ 023 8081 2464
www.furzey-gardens.org
Open daily all year from 10am until dusk. Craft Gallery & Coffee Shop open May to Sept.

MacPennys of Bransgore

154 Burley Road, Bransgore, BH23 8DB
☎ 01425 672348
www.macpennys.co.uk
A 4 acre gravel pit converted into a woodland garden with rare and unusual shrubs, woody and herbaceous plants.

Spinners at Boldre

School Lane, Pilley, Lymington, SO41 5QE
☎ 01590 673 347
www.spinnersgarden.co.uk
A two acre woodland garden which overlooks the Lymington River valley with a good collection of hydrangeas, lilies, hostas and ferns. The nursery sells a very good range of plants and visitors come from far afield for rare hardy plants, trees and shrubs.

The National Gardens Scheme - visitors enjoy access to private gardens which are not normally open to the public and the money raised supports a range of national and local charities. Check website for details: www.ngs.org.uk. There are about twenty gardens which belong to the scheme in the New Forest. Mostly near Fordingbridge, Lymington, Lyndhurst, Ringwood and the Beaulieu River

COUNTRY PARKS

Lepe Country Park

Lepe, Exbury, SO45 1AD
☎ 023 8089 9108
Open 7.30am until dusk all year round. Car Parking charges apply.

Lymington & Keyhaven Nature Reserves

Keyhaven, Nr Lymington
☎ 01590 674656

Accommodation

For all your accommodation needs, please check the official county website:
www.visit-hampshire.co.uk

Cycling

Hampshire offers a wide variety of on and off road cycling opportunities across the county, from the strenuous through to the leisurely, from urban to countryside riding. Once again, Hampshire County Council has an excellent information service, dispensing maps, suggestions and routes. See http://www3.hants.gov.uk/cycling.htm.

Hampshire Farmers Markets

Check website: www.hampshirefarmersmarkets.co.uk

Local Producers of Food, Drinks & Crafts

Check website: www.hampshirefare.co.uk

Useful emails

Hampshire: www.visit-hampshire.co.uk

Winchester: www.visitwinchester.co.uk

Southampton: www.visit-southampton.co.uk

Portsmouth: www.visitportsmouth.co.uk

The New Forest: www.thenewforest.co.uk

Walking

Hampshire provides walkers of all inclinations with almost limitless possibilities and experiences, with opportunities to walk everywhere from chalk downland, river valleys and evocative coastlines to battlefield sites and steeply wooded hills. Well-established, well-maintained footpaths and waymarked routes enable walkers to find their way easily and most paths are accessible at all times of the year, although routes taking in river features and poorly drained, low-lying terrain are generally muddy fom November through to April.

Hampshire County Council has established several long distance footpaths, which are divided into sections of different distances, to cater for walkers of all ages and abilities. Excellent, detailed brochures including maps and describing the individual footpaths and their points of interest en route are available from Tourist Information Centres and as downloads from http://www3.hants.gov.uk/longdistance.

Long Distance Paths

The Avon Valley Path

34 miles (55km). From Salisbury to Christchurch Priory, following the course of the River Avon. The 15-mile (24km) section that runs from Fordingbridge through Ringwood to Sopley is entirely within Hampshire. Parts become seriously waterlogged from Dec to May.

The Hangers Way

21 miles (34km). From Alton to Petersfield, with an extension to finish at Queen Elizabeth Country Park. It takes in several steep-sided wooded hills – called hangers – including the most famous one at Selborne, the home of Gilbert White.

The Solent Way

60 miles (100km). Runs mostly along the coast of Hampshire from Milford-on-Sea around the top of Southampton Water, through Portsmouth, and finally finishes at Emsworth.

The Test Way
44 miles (71km). From Inkpen, just over the border in Berkshire, to follow most of the course of the River Test to Southampton Water.

The Clarendon Way
24 miles (39km. Runs between Winchester and Salisbury, taking in fine countryside in both Wiltshire and Hampshire.

The Staunton Way
8½ or 20½ miles (14 or 33km). Circular route from Queen Elizabeth Country Park, near Petersfield, to Havant. Taking in the varied countryside of Hampshire's eastern border with Sussex.

The Wayfarer's Walk
70 miles (110km). Between the coast at Emsworth and Inkpen Beacon just across the Berkshire border, cutting across the county from south-east to north and taking in a variety of scenery.

St Swithun's Way
34 miles (55km). Between Winchester and Farnham, in imitation of the original medieval pilgrims' route to Canterbury, much of which is now the A31. This alternative route has been chosen for its country setting and opportunities to visit various historic churches on the way.

The South Downs Way
100 miles (160km). From Winchester to Eastbourne in Sussex, with the Hampshire section from Winchester to the West Sussex border just east of Petersfield comprising 28 miles (45km).

Other sections of this unusually effective and informative website have a wide range of shorter walks and topographical details for all parts of the county, together with maps of routes, footpaths and rights of way available as downloads. See http://www3.hants.gov.uk/walking-maps-and-leaflets.htm.

North Hampshire

Boat Trips

Basingstoke Canal Visitors Centre
☎ 01252 370 073
www.basingstoke-canal.co.uk
2½ hour public cruises on the 'John Pinkerton' leave from Fleet and Odiham on Sun Apr–Sept as well as Wed & Fri in the summer holidays. For further details check website: www.johnpinkerton.co.uk ☎ 01962 713564

Events

The Farnborough Air Show
Every two years
www.farnborough.com

Aldershot Army Show
Annual event
www.armyshow.co.uk

Hampshire Food Festival
Annual event
www.hampshirefare.co.uk/food-festival

Other Markets
Tuesdays: Farnborough, Odiham
Wednesdays: Basingstoke, Hartley Wintney
Thursdays: Aldershot, Andover
Fridays: Whitchurch
Saturdays: Andover, Basingstoke, Fleet

Winchester and the Centre

Events

Alresford Show
Annual event
www.alresfordshow.co.uk

Alton Show
Annual event
www.altonshow.co.uk

Winchester Christmas Market
Annual event
www.winchesterchristmasmarket.co.uk

Winchester Festival
Annual event
www.winchesterfestival.co.uk

Hampshire Food Festival
Annual event
www.hampshirefare.co.uk/food-festival

Other Markets
Tuesdays: Alton
Wednesdays: Winchester
Thursdays: New Alresford, Winchester
Fridays: Winchester
Saturdays: Winchester

Southampton

Activity Centres

Woodmill Outdoor Activities Centre
Woodmill Lane, Swaythling, SO18 2JR
☎ 023 8091 5746
www.woodmill.co.uk
For course details and prices see website.

Southampton Alpine Centre
Sports Centre, Bassett, SO16 7AY
☎ 023 8078 2291
www.southampton-alpine-centre.co.uk
For facilities and prices see website.

Airport
Southampton Airport is located to the north of junction 5 of the M27. The nearest railway station is Southampton Parkway which is 100 metres from the airport.
For further details check the website www.southamptonairport.com

Fact File

Boat Trips

Red Funnel
Dock Gate 7, off Town Quay Road, SO14 2AQ
☎ 0844 844 9988
www.redfunnel.co.uk
One hour vehicle ferry crossing from Southampton to East Cowes on the Isle of Wight. 24 hour service. The Red Jet Hi-Speed foot passenger service to West Cowes also on Town Quay operates from 5.45am–11.45pm (20 minute crossing).

Blue Funnel Boat Trips
Ocean Village, SO14 3TJ
☎ 023 80 223278
www.bluefunnel.co.uk
Boat trip excursions to Rivers Itchen, Test, Beaulieu and Hamble, the Isle of Wight, the 'Scenic Solent' and to view the cruise ships. For details and prices see website.

Events

Southampton Boat Show
Held in Sept every year
www.southamptonboatshow

The Romsey Show
Every year
www.romseyshow.co.uk

Other Markets
Tuesdays: Romsey
Fridays: Romsey, Southampton
Saturdays: Romsey

Shopping Centre

West Quay Shopping Centre
☎ 023 8033 6828
www.west-quay.co.uk

Portsmouth

Activity Centres

Peter Ashley Activity Centre
Fort Purbrook, Portsdown Hill Road, Farlington, PO6 1BJ
☎ 023 9232 1223
www.peterashleyactivitycentres.co.uk
For activity details please check website.

The Pyramids
Clarence Esplanade, Southsea, PO5 3ST
☎ 023 9279 9977
www.pyramids.co.uk
For opening times and prices check website.

The Mountbatten Leisure Centre
Alexandra Park, Portsmouth, PO2 9QA
☎ 023 9262 6500
www.leisurecentre.com/centres/34/home/The-Mountbatten-Centre
Open daily. For facilities, swimming pool opening times and prices check website.

Boat Trips

Gosport Ferry Ltd
Bus Station, South St, Gosport, PO12 1EP
☎ 023 92524551
www.gosportferry.co.uk
A five minute ferry service from Gosport to Portsmouth. Every day except Christmas Day.
From 5.30am–midnight, weather permitting. For details see website.

Hamble to Warsash Ferry
The Ferry Hard, Hamble, SO31 4JB
☎ 023 8045 4512
www.hamble-warsashferry.co.uk
Summer 9am–6pm, Winter 9am–4pm.

Hovertravel
Clarence Esplanade, Southsea, PO5 3AD
☎ 023 92 811000
www.hovertravel.co.uk
Approx 12 minute crossing to Ryde Esplanade. Mon–Fri from 6.30am–9.20pm (from
8.30am on Sat & 8am on Sun).

Solent and Wightline Cruises Ltd
43 Hamilton Rd, Ryde, Isle of Wight, PO33 3QY
☎ 01983 564602
www.solentcruises.co.uk
Portsmouth Harbour cruises from Portsmouth Historic Dockyard and Gunwharf Quays.

Wightlink Car Ferry
Gunwharf Road, Portsmouth, PO1 2LA
☎ 0871 376 1000
www.wightlink.co.uk
40 minute vehicle ferry crossing to Fishbourne on the Isle of Wight.

Wightlink Fast Cat
Portsmouth Harbour Station, The Hard, P01 3PS
☎ 0871 376 1000
www.wightlink.co.uk
18 minute crossing to Ryde Pierhead on the Isle of Wight. For details see website.

Continental Ferryport Portsmouth
Brittany Ferries, Condor Ferries, LD Lines and P&O operate ferries from Portsmouth to
France, Spain and the Channel Islands.

Events

Festival of Christmas
Annual event
Portsmouth Historic Dockyard
www.christmasfestival.co.uk

Hollycombe Steam Rally
Annual event
www.hollycombe.co.uk/special_events

The Garden Show
Every June at Stansted Park
www.thegardenshowonline.com

Other Markets

Mondays: Fareham
Tuesdays: Gosport, Havant
Wednesdays: Portchester, Petersfield

Thursdays: Portsmouth , Waterlooville
Saturdays: Portsmouth, Gosport, Havant,
Petersfield

Retail Outlet Centres

Gunwharf Quays
☎ 023 9283 6700
www.gunwharf-quays.com

Whiteley Village
Whiteley Way, Whiteley, PO15 7LJ
☎ 01489 886886
www.whiteleyvillage.com

The New Forest

Activity Centres

Calshot Activities Centre
Calshot Spit, Fawley SO45 1BR
☎ 023 8089 2077
www.calshot.com.
For courses and opening times check website.

Boat Trips
Hythe Ferry Office, Prospect Place, Hythe, SO45 6AU
☎ 023 8084 0722
www.hytheferry.co.uk
Hythe Ferry runs daily except Christmas Day and Boxing Day.

Beaulieu River
Bucklers Hard, SO42 7XB. Follow brown tourist signs.
☎ 01590 614645
www.bucklershard.co.uk
30 minute river cruise operates from Buckler's Hard between Easter and October.

Wightlink Car Ferry
Lymington Pier, Undershore Road, Lymington, SO41 5SB
☎ 0871 376 4342
www.wightlink.co.uk
30 minute vehicle ferry crossing from Lymington to Yarmouth on the Isle of Wight. 24 hour service.

Keyhaven - Hurst Castle Ferry
☎ 07766 310751 or ☎ 07802 503678
www.hurstcastle.co.uk
This ferry operates seasonally. For further details please check website.

Events

The New Forest Show
(The end of July every year)
New Park, Near Brockenhurst SO42 7QH
www.newforestshow.co.uk
For further details check website.

Other Markets
Tuesdays: Hythe

Wednesdays: Ringwood, New Milton

Saturdays: Lymington

Index

A

Action Stations, Portsmouth 90
Adjutant General's Corps Museum,
    Winchester 56
Aldershot 17
Aldershot Military Museum 32
Alice Holt Forest 111,121
Allen Gallery, Alton 55
Alton 50
Andover 26
Andover Museum 32
Apple Court at Hordle 136
Archaeology Museum,
    Southampton 65
Ashmansworth 30
Ashurst 130
Avington 48
Avington Church 46
Avington Park 48,55
Avon Heath Country Park 132
Avon Valley Path 132

B

Bargate, Southampton 63
Basing House 21,32
Basingstoke Canal 22
Beacon Hill 29
Beaulieu 128
Beaulieu Abbey Ruins 135
Birdworld, Nr Farnham 111,119
Bishop's Waltham 54
Bishop's Waltham Palace 55
Blashford Lakes Nature Reserve 132
Block Mills, Portsmouth 91
Blue Reef Aquarium, Portsmouth
    93,119
Boarhunt 97
Bolderwood Arboretum Ornamental
    Drive 131
Bolderwood Deer Sanctuary 131,135
Boldre 125
Botley 73
Bramley 24
Bramshaw Commons 130
Bramshott 109
Branksome China 133,135
Breamore 134
Breamore Countryside Museum 134
Breamore House 134
Broadlands, Romsey 67,68,76
Brockenhurst 125
Bucklers Hard 10,127,135
Burghclere 28
Buriton 108
Burley 132
Bursledon Brickworks 105
Bursledon Windmill 105,119
Butser Ancient Farm 107,119
Butser Hill 107

C

Cadnam 130
Calshot Castle 135
Canadian Memorial, New Forest 131

Canute's Palace , Southampton 64
Chalton 108
Chapel of the Holy Ghost, The,
    Basingstoke 21
Charles Dickens Birthplace Museum,
    Portsmouth 95,119
Chawton 52
Cheriton 49
Chilbolton Cow Common 31
City Mill, Winchester 55
City Museum, Portsmouth 119
Civic Centre Art Gallery, Southampton
    66
Clarence Pier, Portsmouth 92
Crondall 17
Crookham 23
Curtis Museum, Alton 52

D

D-Day Museum 93,119
Danebury Hill Fort 32
Dockyard Apprentices Museum,
    Portsmouth 90
Domus Dei, Portsmouth 85
Dummer 24

E

East Meon 115
East Wellow 66
Eling Tide Mill 135
Ellingham 133
Emery Down 131
Emsworth 113
Exbury Gardens 136
Explosion! The Museum of Naval
    Firepower, Gosport 101,119
Eyeworth Pond 130

F

Fareham 100
Farley Mount Country Park 46,57
Farlington Marshes 95
Farnborough 15
Farnborough Airshow 15
Fleet Pond Local Nature Reserve 16
Fordingbridge 133
Fort Brockhurst, Gosport 102,119
Fort Nelson, Nr Fareham 98
Fritham 130
Funland Amusement Park,
    Hayling Island 120
Furzey Gardens 131,136

G

Gilbert White's House & the Oates
    Museum, Selborne 10,120
Go Ape, Ringwood 135
God's House Tower Museum of
    Archaeology, Southampton 65,76
Gosport 100
Great Hall, Winchester 56
Guardroom Museum 44
Gunwharf Quays 89
Gurkha Museum, Winchester 44

H

Hamble 106
Hambledon 118
Hartley Wintney 18
Havant 111
Hawk Conservancy Trust,
    Nr Andover 27,32
Hayling Island 113
Highclere Castle 11,32
Hinton Ampner 49,55
HMS Victory, Portsmnouth 85
HMS Warrior 1860, Portsmouth 87
Hollycombe Steam Collection,
    Liphook 111,120
Horsepower Museum, Winchester
    44,57
Hospital of St Cross, Winchester 56
Houghton Lodge Gardens &
    Hydroponicum 77
Hurstbourne Tarrant 30
Hurst Castle, Keyhaven 126,135
Hyde Abbey, Winchester 45

I

Idsworth 108
Intech Science Centre & Planetarium,
    Winchester 45,56
Itchen Valley Country Park 77

J

Jane Austen's House, Chawton 55

K

Keyhaven 126
King John's House, Romsey 69,76

L

Langstone 111
Laverstoke 25
Lee-on-the-Solent 102
Lepe Country Park 136
Liberty's Owl, Raptor & Reptile
    Centre, Ringwood 132,135
Longdown Activity Farm, Ashurst
    130,135
Longstock Water Garden 72,77
Lymington 125
Lymington & Keyhaven Nature
    Reserves 126,136

M

MacPennys of Bransgore 136
Manor Farm Country Park 106,121
Maritime Museum, Southampton
    64,76,128
Maritime Museum, Buckler's Hard
    128
Martin Peninsula 134
Marwell Wildlife 55
Mary Rose, Portsmouth 88
Mayflower Park, Southampton 64
Medieval Merchant's House,
    Southampton 66,76
Middle Wallop 28

Index

Milestones, Basingstoke   11,20,32
Milford on Sea   126
Military Museum, Aldershot   18
Minstead   131
Moors Valley Country Park   132
Mottisfont Abbey and Gardens   77
Museum of Army Flying,
    Middle Wallop   28,32
Museum of the Iron Age, Andover   26,32

N

National Garden Scheme   33, 57, 77, 121, 136
National Motor Museum, Beaulieu   128,135
Natural History Museum, Portsmouth   94,120
Naval Memorial, Portsmouth   93
Nether Wallop   28
Netley Abbey   73,76
Netley Castle   74
New Forest and Hampshire County Show   124
New Forest Centre   135
New Forest Otter, Owl & Wildlife Park   130,135
New Forest Reptile Centre   131,136
New Milton   126
Norman House, Southampton   64
Northington Grange, Alresfortd   48,55

O

Ocean Village, Southampton   66
Odiham   17
Odiham Castle   17,18
Old Basing   20
Old Portsmouth   80,82
Old Winchester Hill   117

P

Palace House, Beaulieu   135
Pamber   23
Paulton's Park, Ower   72,76
Petersfield   108
Piper's Wait   122
Portchester   95
Portchester Castle   10,96,120
Portsmouth   80-95
Portsmouth Guildhall   95
Portsmouth Historic Dockyard   10,85-89,120
Port Solent Marina   95
Pyramids, Southsea   93

Q

Quay Hill, Lymington   125
Queen's Eleanor's Garden, Winchester   57
Queen Elizabeth Country Park, Nr Petersfield   107,121

R

Rhinefield Ornamental Drive   125

Ringwood   132
Ringwood Brewery   132
River Hamble   105
River Meon   114
Rifles Museum, Winchester   44,56
Rockbourne Roman Villa   133,136
Roman Catholic Cathedral, Portsmouth   82
Romsey   67
Romsey Abbey   70,76
Round Tower, Old Portsmouth   83
Royal Armouries Museum at Fort Nelson, Nr Fareham   120
Royal Hampshire Regiment Museum, Winchester   57
Royal Green Jackets Museum, Winchester
Royal Marines Museum, Portsmouth   94,120
Royal Naval Museum, Portsmouth   88
Royal Navy Submarine Museum, Gosport   101,120
Royal Victoria Country Park   74,77
Rufus Stone, Nr Cadnam   130

S

Sammy Miller Motorcycle Museum, New Milton   136
Sandham Memorial Chapel   29,32
Selborne   109
Silchester   24
Silk Mill, Whitchurch   33
Sir Harold Hiller Garden, Ampfield   77
Soberton   117
Solent Way   105
Southampton   59
Southampton Hall of Aviation (Solent Sky)   65
Southampton Town Walls   62
South Parade Pier, Southsea   93
Southsea   91
Southsea Castle   92,121
Southsea seafront   81
Southwick   98
Sparsholt   46
Spinnaker Tower, Portsmouth   89,121
Spinners at Boldre   136
Spitbank Fort   121
Spur Redoubt, Old Portsmouth   83
Square Tower, Old Portsmouth   83
Stansted Park   121
Staunton Country Park   121
St Barbe Museum & Art Gallery, Lymington   126,136
Stella Memorial, Southampton   64
Steventon   25
St John the Baptist, Winchester   45
St Mary's Church, Portchester   97
St Michael's Abbey, Farnborough   16,32
St Michael's Church, Basingstoke   20
St Michael's Church, Southampton   65
Stockbridge   71
Stokes Bay   102

Stratfield Saye House   32
Sutton Scotney   46

T

Thruxton   28
Tichborne   48
Titchfield Abbey   77,104,121
Titchfield Haven National Nature Reserve   121
Town Quay, Southampton   64
Tudor House Museum, Southampton   65,77
Tudor Merchant's Hall, Southampton   64

V

Viables Craft Centre, Basingstoke   33
Victoria Park, Portsmouth   95
The Vyne, Sherborne St John   23,33

W

Warnford   116
Warsash   105
Watercress Line   144
Watership Down   29
Wellington Country Park   11
Wellington Statue   17,18
Westbury Manor Museum, Fareham   100,121
Westgate Museum, Winchester   43,56
West Green House   19
West Meon   115
Wherwell   31
Whitchurch   25
Whitchurch Silk Mill   33
Wickham   117
Willis Museum, Basingstoke   20
Winchester   34
Winchester Castle   41
Winchester Cathedral   37,56
Winchester College   40,56
Wolverton Church   25
Wolvesey Castle, Winchester   40,56

Y

Yateley Country Park   33